Minister's Manual

Edited by John Rempel

Faith & Life Press
Newton, Kansas
Winnipeg, Manitoba

Herald Press
Scottdale, Pennsylvania
Waterloo, Ontario

Most of the hymns and some of the readings in this manual are found in *Hymnal: A Worship Book,* published in 1992 by Faith & Life Press, Herald Press and Brethren Press. *Hymanal: A Worship Book* is abbreviated as HWB.

Patterns and Prayer for Christian Worship, (Oxford, England: Oxford University Press, 1991), *Book of Common Prayer,* (New York, Church Pension Fund, 1979) and *For All Who Minister* (Elgin: Brethren Press, 1993) were valuable sources of information to the compilers of this *Minister's Manual.*

Printed in the United States of America

International Standard Book Number 0-87303-320-5
Library of Congress Number 97-76991

Editorial direction by Susan E. Janzen; copyediting by Mary L. Gaeddert; design by John Hiebert

Scripture text from the New Revised Standard Version, copyright © 1990, Division of Christian Education of the National Council of the Churches of Christ in the United States of America.

Contents

Introduction

"Where the Spirit of the Lord is, there is freedom" (2 Cor. 3:17). That is the first thought which comes to mind to introduce the Minister's Manual. It is the work of many hands, words lovingly gathered in order to be scattered again with imagination and freedom. These words come alive in the presence of the Holy Spirit, but they come to us through the tradition that began with the Exodus. Words that were spoken and signs that were offered take on life across the centuries every time they give utterance to our relationship with God. They name the dreams, signs, and wonders sent to us from the past. In worship these words burst with redeeming power. There are many words in this book, ancient and modern. They express the faith, hope, and charity of God's people in biblical times, of the whole Christian church, and of the Mennonite church beginning with the sixteenth century. But the tradition they represent is open-ended. Every time a congregation gathers for worship, it re-ignites and reshapes the inheritance to express its praise and petitions.

The custom of creating worship resources for ministers and congregations in our denomination goes back at least to 1625 when Leonard Clock published a booklet of eighteen prayers. Through the centuries, those prayers were copied by hand and circulated and finally incorporated into the *Prayer Book for Earnest Christians*.[2] Other more extensive manuals were published. These too were copied in manuscript form and adapted to new circumstances in the process. There were also times and settings in which manuscripts were put aside, and fresh words were received from the Spirit. But even in eras when prayer books were put aside, their most haunting and consoling phrases were retained in the communal memory.

As it turned out, Mennonites found two ways of shaping their inner voice. Prayer books guided their devotion, but were freely altered and even discarded. Renewal movements brought fresh experiences and words of grace, but precisely because they too were treasured, these new words were memorized and often committed to writing. This is how the Holy Spirit teaches the church: by making old words come alive, by shaping them for a new era, and by bursting into the church with novel words that come straight from the heart. This is the pattern that all communities of faith experience. In preparing this Minister's Manual, we have placed our work within the larger flow of the Spirit's ministry. The words before you stand at the outset of a worship leader's task. All of them may be adapted and transcended. Their preparation will have been worthwhile if they can be the starting point for a congregation's praise.

Those who prepared this book have steeped themselves in Mennonite ways of worship and studied past Minister's Manuals for treasured and usable worship resources. This manual has been written in a time of religious and social upheaval as great as that of the Reformation. Like the Christians of that age, we find inherited spiritual categories inadequate to our experience of God and the world. Therefore, we have borrowed widely—from Judaism, from the ancient church in East and West, from the Middle Ages, from the Reformation, from Pietism, and from the ecumenical movement throughout the present world.

A word should be said concerning the categories we chose for these materials. Our goal was to provide words and actions that bring all of our life as individuals, churches, and the world before God. We have included obvious categories like baptism and the Lord's Supper. In addition to that, we have grouped acts of blessing in a common class to make their role clear. A wedding is an act of blessing, but so also is a benediction for someone newly widowed or separated. Likewise, there is a category for healing and lament which includes diverse actions like funerals and anointings. One difficult section is included—congregational discernment, including binding and loosing—because old forms are worn out, yet there is a cry for authentic ways of speaking to these challenging aspects of congregational life.

Mennonites have a strong sense of church. We remember that we belong to the communion of saints, the church of the living and the dead. This means that our worship crosses lines of time, culture, and tradition. It means that no one cultural expression of worship, whether it be traditional German or contemporary North American, fully expresses all of our life in God. This fact prompts some people to suggest dispensing with written worship resources all together. But we need a book because we have a story. The most profound contribution of this book to Mennonite worship in this generation, God willing, will be to convey to congregations the sense that they belong to the communion of saints, and that their words and gestures and music extend through Christ around the world and back to the calling of Israel. If traditional Mennonites, those fed by the liturgical movement, and those inspired by the charismatic movement can all see themselves as part of a church that is more than the sum of its parts, we will discern a worship life in which the traditions live and merge because the Spirit enables new ways.

I would like to thank the committee that oversaw the creation of this manual, wrote initial drafts of essays and resources, and critiqued each stage of the process. Susan Janzen and Marlene Kropf led the committee whose members were Dave Bergen, Tom Kauffman, Andrew Kreider, Dorothy Nickel Friesen, Sue Steiner, and John

Rempel. John Esau made valuable contributions to the process. On their behalf, I am grateful to all those who offered us their prayers or wrote them for our use. My heartfelt thanks go to my two bosses, Manhattan Mennonite Fellowship and Robert Herr of the Mennonite Central Committee Peace Office, for the time and encouragement they gave me to carry out this unexpected project. In addition, I want to acknowledge three ministers whose worship leading and preaching shaped my experience of God profoundly: Frank C. Peters, Ottawa St. Mennonite Brethren Church, Kitchener, Ontario; Walter Klaassen, Conrad Grebel College, Waterloo, Ontario; and John H. Mosemann, College Mennonite Church, Goshen, Indiana. Their voices are heard on these pages. I am grateful to John Plummer not only for his expert typing skills, but also for his liturgical and literary prowess. I can think of no greater honor than the one I received in being asked to edit this volume, that of listening for and giving expression to the voice of a people at prayer, my people.

May this book unite us with the living Triune God in our midst, and with the Church in all times and places. May it make us fearless, passionate, and openhearted friends and followers of Christ.

John Rempel, editor[1]
July 1997
New York City

Worship and Ritual

Christian worship is the church's offering of love and praise to God. Like the woman who poured fragrant perfume on Jesus' head (Mt. 26:6-13), worshipers honor Christ when they give their heart's adoration in response to God's lavish gifts of mercy and grace. In the acts of worship, Christians are inspired, renewed, and transformed by the Holy Spirit to live and serve as God's faithful people in the world.

Throughout Christian history, the weekly Sunday worship of Christians has consisted of similar elements: praying, singing, reading Scripture, preaching or teaching, offering gifts, and celebrating the Lord's Supper. When *Hymnal: A Worship Book*[3] was being compiled, members of the Worship Committee conducted a survey of church bulletins produced by General Conference Mennonite, Mennonite, and Church of the Brethren congregations throughout Canada and the United States to determine what elements of worship were commonly included and what order of worship was typical. The results of the survey provided a framework for organizing the contents of the 1992 hymnal.

In simplified form, the typical actions of worship can be described as follows:

• GATHERING: Being invited into the presence of God through preparatory music, a visual focus, a call to worship or greeting, hymns of gathering, a procession, or an opening prayer;

- PRAISING GOD: Offering praise and adoration through hymns and songs of praise, Scripture readings (especially the Psalms) or other responsive readings or prayers;
- CONFESSING AND RECONCILING: Acknowledging our need of God's grace and mercy through sung or spoken prayers of confession or silence; receiving cleansing and forgiveness through words of assurance, simple rituals of reconciliation, or songs celebrating God's grace;
- OFFERING OURSELVES AND OUR GIFTS: Giving gifts (money or other symbols) representing the commitment of our whole lives to Christ's service through the offering of money, music, silence, dance, or processions;
- HEARING GOD'S WORD: Listening to God's Word to us through Scripture reading, preaching or teaching, drama, dance, music, or other worship arts;
- RESPONDING TO THE WORD: Affirming our faith in sung or spoken words, personal testimonies, prayers of thanksgiving, intercession and petition, celebrating communion (on communion Sundays), or other rituals of response;
- SENDING: Receiving a sung or spoken blessing or benediction as empowerment for ministry in the world.

A biblical foundation for these acts of worship can be found in a passage such as Isaiah 6:1-8 in which the prophet beholds a vision of God's glory in the temple. The first action of worship is a response of praise and adoration offered to God; it is followed by an act of confession and cleansing; then the worshiper is prepared to hear God's Word anew and to respond in faith and obedience.

These basic actions of worship, which may be expressed in a wide variety of patterns and styles influenced by local culture and tradition, form the foundation not only for regular weekly worship but also for ritual occasions such as baptism, communion, weddings, or funerals. In other words, the same actions of worship included in a typical Sunday service will also be found in a special service on a ritual occasion. A baptismal service or communion service is an extension of the congregation's ordinary worship and usually includes, for example, a time of gathering and sending as well as offerings of praise, acts of confession, hearing the Word, and responding to the Word.

To facilitate the planning of worship for special ritual occasions, a helpful set of questions to ask is:

What face of God shines upon the congregation on this occasion?

What particular characteristic of God's activity

>   *illuminates worship on this day?*
>
>   *What is God doing in the midst of the ritual?*
>
>   *What change or transformation is occurring for the human actors in the midst of the ritual?*
>
>   *What is the expected outcome or consequence of the ritual?*

For example, in a funeral service, worshipers are often keenly aware of God's faithfulness or their need for God's comforting presence. They desire support and assurance of God's care so they can face the future with trust. At a wedding, the congregation may be particularly conscious of God's love graciously expressed in covenant relationships. Two people become one as they are united in God's love and look forward to creating a new home where Christ rules and reigns. In a baptismal service, people remember God as the giver of new life, the one who cleanses and forgives, and the one who creates a new community. The believer being baptized is raised from death to life, becomes a member of the family of faith, and receives the power of the Spirit to follow Christ's way in the world. If worship planners and leaders are careful to identify the particular face or characteristic of God present in the ritual and the change being effected, appropriate Scriptures and music choices will not be difficult to find.

Rituals in worship offer three gifts to the people of God:

1. They offer a secure framework of order and stability in which something new occurs. In a wedding, a new union is created; in baptism, a new Christian emerges; at a funeral, a soul is released into God's eternal care. Because of this function, rituals need to include a recital of God's faithful, loving acts in the past, which form a sturdy foundation for hope in the future. It is also important for leaders to use the same or similar words and phrases each time rituals are repeated in order to establish this framework of order and stability.

2. They establish bonds of love and unity among the people of God. A vibrant sense of community is nourished and enhanced when worshipers purposefully participate in the rituals of worship and join with God's actions.

3. They create a vision of God's new future and empower people to live with courage and joy as they anticipate the fulfillment of God's reign. Appropriate symbols help to convey a sense of hope and expectation for the future.

Worship rituals normally include both words and actions. In an ordination service, the leader says, "I ordain you...," while at the same time placing hands of blessing on the person being ordained. In the same way, in a baptismal service, the leader says, "I baptize you...," while water is poured on the believer or the believer is immersed in water. A commonly stated guideline for rituals is "Good ritual doesn't love paper." What this means is that the more freely leaders and the congregation can participate in rituals, the more powerful they will be. Because the actions of rituals are critical, it is important for everyone to be as unencumbered as possible to join in the action, not having heads down and eyes glued to paper. For this reason, leaders of ritual are encouraged to memorize the most important words and phrases in frequently enacted rituals.

Three groups of people are essential in a ritual: the congregation, its leaders, and the person or persons who are the center of the ritual. Leaders of ritual fulfill a priestly role in the congregation, bringing people into the presence of God and invoking God's blessing in the midst of ritual actions. The congregation fulfills a critical role as they affirm God's blessing and offer love and support. Those who are the center of the ritual need to be encouraged to be receptive and open to the movement of God's Spirit. It is God, of course, who is the most important actor in any ritual; what the human actors do is simply become vessels through which the grace, healing, and blessing of God can flow in worship.

To designate roles in worship we have used the simple designations "L" (leader) and "P" (people) throughout.

Worship Beyond Words

Words are central to many aspects of worship. God speaks to us through the Bible and through the Word proclaimed. We, in turn, speak to God through prayers and hymns. At the heart of these activities is our desire to find a place in which we can meet God, a sacred space. Such a holy space, however, is not limited to the realm of words. In many instances, our experience of God is beyond words, and we can respond to this reality by including nonverbal elements in our worship.

Worship beyond words can take many creative forms, traditional and modern, including the arts, physical gestures, and silence. These elements bring people to meet God in a way that cannot be expressed only in words. Such symbols can be stimulating and meaningful, but also distracting or even disruptive. They can hinder people from meeting God rather than creating a space for such a meeting. Thus in considering the use of these elements in our worship, we need to test our ideas: Are the symbols we use, or are proposing to use, appropriate to the theme of our worship? Do they fit into the flow of our worship? Are they appropriate for public worship? Do they help us to meet God?

The Senses in Worship
Many Christians use powerful physical symbols

to communicate the presence of God. Communion and baptism, for example, are rich in symbolism; they are the root signs of the gospel. All other signs derive from and refer to the realities acted out in the two primal ceremonies. In baptism, we use water to represent the cleansing from sin, the dying and rising of the person being baptized. At communion, we use the bread and cup to symbolize the body and blood of Jesus. In some churches, oil is used for anointing the sick and ordaining ministers to communicate God's healing and sustaining presence. In all these cases, our actions combine with our words in an offering of worship. This act of communication works in two directions, for just as we reach out to God through nonverbal means, God is also present with us in ways beyond words.

The realms of sight and smell are powerful media for communicating an experience of God beyond words. Some churches use ordinary objects to represent God's presence with us. The most basic of these are the Lord's table and a baptismal vessel. The table has (or should have) a prominent place. Permanently displaying a baptismal vessel, where immersion is practiced, by building a visible, accessible baptistry can make covenant and cleansing a more vivid part of worship life and let newcomers know at a glance what this community is based on. Various specific objects can intensify the encounter with God and

God's people. A large stone can be used as a memorial object once a year, like the Ebenezer stone set up by Samuel (1 Sam. 7:12). A table, carefully decorated, can enhance the theme of the worship. Some churches use banners and wall hangings to highlight a theme or season of worship. Others use candles or stained glass to create a visual sacred space in which to encounter God. These visual signs are often most powerful when they contain no words, for then they open us up to God's presence without limiting themselves to the boundaries of a text. Smell can also lead us into worship. The odor of freshly baked bread or an arrangement of flowers in a meeting place can invite us into God's presence. Strong smells, however, need to be treated with care, for they also can affect people with allergies.

We can use our bodies to express our response to God. Some churches do this by kneeling or standing during the prayers or by standing when the gospel is read. Other churches have the congregation come to the front to present their offerings, while still others use movement and dance. Involving our bodies in worship takes us beyond words and allows us to respond to God with our whole beings.

Music
Mennonites have a rich heritage in music, and music is an important part of worship for many

Mennonite congregations. Much of our theology is expressed in our hymns, and the act of singing together also affirms our solidarity as a body of believers. The early Anabaptists sang in unison in a style still retained by the Amish today. In the nineteenth century, Mennonites organized singing schools in churches and took up the four-part harmony style that is common in many churches today. *Hymnal: A Worship Book* incorporates songs and hymns from many countries and traditions, including both unison songs and four-part hymns.

Music is the most prevalent example of the establishment of a sacred space beyond words in our worship. Alongside congregational singing, there is also room for special music played or sung by groups or individuals as an offering to God on behalf of the whole congregation. The experience of hearing instrumental music can also open a wordless space in which we meet God. People's understandable desire for intensity of experience in worship sometimes becomes a demand that they be made to feel good. That is when worship shades off into entertainment. Applause (which is different from clapping in time to the music) is often more an acknowledgement of feeling good than of being in the presence of God.

Silence

Silence is a necessary balance for congregations whose worship incorporates many words. It can be the most intimate setting in which we meet God and is also perhaps the hardest element to manage in a congregational setting. Silence opens a space for God to speak in our hearts and for us to listen to God. Silence needs to be introduced with care in worship, for not everyone is comfortable with it. Children and adults alike can handle silence well, but often they first need to understand why no words are being spoken. Carefully introduced, silence can bring moments of deep listening to God and an open space in our worship in which God's Spirit can move. One fruitful time of silence is immediately after the sermon.

Exploring the symbolism in our present forms of worship and developing fresh symbols and forms to complement these can deepen our experience of God and lead us anew into the rich dimensions of worship without words.

The Church at Prayer

The Minister's Life of Prayer

As ministers, our own life of prayer undergirds our ministry. Our own relationship with God provides the deep center that empowers our ministry. When we are refreshed by streams of living water, we can offer God's refreshment to others as we engage in our work as pastor and priest.

A life of prayer means being alert to God's movement in all situations—honing the ability to notice God in the normal joys and struggles of our humanness. It means being conscious of a loving God who delights in relating to us.

Our relationship with God is nourished and deepened as we commit ourselves to various prayer disciplines—some of them practiced daily, some weekly, and others at periodic intervals. These disciplines will vary from pastor to pastor and from time to time—depending on our own personality, our lived history of relating to God, our family situation, and other factors.

Our own spiritual disciplines as ministers must be differentiated from studying a Bible passage in order to prepare a sermon or shaping a pastoral prayer for the congregation. Here we approach Scripture not to exegete it, but for it to exegete us. As we pray with Scripture, we descend with our mind into our heart. We read a short passage slowly and meditatively. Perhaps we wait for a word or phrase to address us. Perhaps we enter a gospel scene imaginatively, finding our place in relation to Jesus and dialoguing with him. After a time of communing with God in Scripture, we might offer prayers of thanksgiving and confession. We might release to God concerns for our work in prayers of intercession and discernment.

In addition to praying with Scripture, some of us pray while walking early in the morning or late at night. Others pray via the texts and tunes of favorite hymns and spiritual songs (hymns are a basic expression of spirituality for many Mennonites). Still others read spiritual classics or follow lectionary-based resources such as *A Guide to Prayer for Ministers and Other Servants*.[4] Some worship through a simple format of morning and/or evening prayer. Others find it essential to do a self-examination at the end of each day, noticing the movements of God in our life by asking questions such as: What am I most grateful for today? least grateful? How does that lead me to thanksgiving, confession, intercession, and discernment? Still others write in a prayer journal daily or during a longer weekly period of prayer and reflection. Some have incorporated periods of fasting as a spiritual discipline. Others take a retreat day monthly and/or a longer retreat time annually—a time set apart from our ministry setting and the demands of family for a sustained period of prayer, leading us back to a clearer focus on God.

Many ministers find it helpful, if not essential, to be accountable to someone else in our life with God. Some do this with a spiritual friend, sharing weekly or monthly in a reciprocal way. Others meet with a spiritual accountability group of peers in ministry. Still others have an ongoing relationship with a spiritual director or arrange for direction while on retreat. Some such relationship helps keep us from self-deception and gives us a safe place to share our doubts, dry spells, and confusions.

However we go about it, the best way we can ensure faithful service to our God and our congregation is to attend to our own life of prayer, and let God shape our ministry through it. The prayer resources that follow may be used by ministers for individual private prayer as well as for public worship.

Daily Prayer

Daily prayer includes occasions that happen in the course of an ordinary day when people gather formally and informally in prayer. The custom of regular private and public prayer time each day goes back at least to temple and synagogue piety in Judaism long before Christ. Jesus and the earliest church participated in these prayer times. Eventually it became customary for all Christians who were able to gather in a locality to begin and end the day together in prayer. During the Middle Ages, this practice became more and more confined to religious orders and clergy. But morning and evening prayer for the congregation were part of the worship renewal of the Reformation. Because Mennonites had no secure meeting places for a long time, these devotions were largely carried out at home. From the early 1600s, there are collections of Mennonite prayer books with prayers for morning and evening.[5]

Leonard Clock, a Mennonite minister and writer at the end of the sixteenth century, wrote that he had composed prayers for public worship which he also intended as models for private devotion. The resources presented in this section have that multiple intention. Their first purpose is to guide groups of people who gather—for morning and evening prayer, prayer meetings, retreats, and church committees. Their second purpose is to guide families and households. Their third purpose is to guide individuals in their devotions. We hope that ministers in particular can adapt these resources to their various pastoral roles and needs.

It is inspiring to recall that we never pray alone. This is graphically illustrated by the fact that when we gather at a specific time of day, others throughout our time zone are also doing so. And as we conclude our offering, Christians in the next time zone are beginning theirs.

Prayer Services and Resources
Outline of Daily Prayer

Hymn (a single lit candle or group of candles can be
an effective reminder of the presence of Christ. The
light of morning or evening prayer)

Opening response or traditional morning or evening
prayer

Scripture (a psalm and a reading from the Old or New
Testament)

Silence

Optional brief commentary on the readings by the
leader and/or participants

Hymn

Intercessory prayer (focusing especially on the reason
for gathering) may conclude with the Lord's Prayer

Sending (this and the hymn could come at the end of
the event, if the reason for gathering is a meeting)

Hymn

Service of Morning Prayer

Morning hymn (HWB 644-651)

Opening Response

L: O Lord, open my lips.

P: And my mouth shall proclaim your praise.

L: I pray to you, O Lord;

P: You hear my voice in the morning;

L: at sunrise I offer my prayer

P: and wait for your answer.[6]

Psalm and Bible reading

Silence

Commentary (optional)

Hymn or scriptural song of response

Intercessions (free prayers and/or silence following each petition)

P: Gracious God, grant us your Holy Spirit that we might pray according to your will.

L: For the church in all places and for every ministry each of us has received from Christ.

L: For this gathering.

L: For the peace of the world.

L: For those in positions of public trust.

L: For all human labor.

L: For those in poverty, danger, sorrow, and suffering.

L: For enemies.

L: For ourselves, that Christ might be first in our hearts.

All: Almighty God, you have given us grace

at this time with one accord to make our common supplications to you, and you have promised through your well-beloved Son that when two or three are gathered together you will hear their requests. Fulfill now our desires and petitions, as may be best for us, granting us in this world knowledge of your truth, and in the age to come eternal life, through Jesus Christ our Lord. Amen.[7]

Sending

L: This is the day that the Lord has made.
P: We will rejoice and be glad in it.
L: Go in peace and serve the Lord.
P: We will seek peace and pursue it.
All: Amen.[8] *If you wish to copy, contact G.I.A. Publications, phone 708 / 496-3800.*

Hymn

A Service of Sung Evening Prayer

A forty-five to sixty-minute sung evening prayer service can be a fitting way to close a conference or other church gathering. Such a service invites people to give thanks, offer their concerns to God, and rest in the comfort of God's care. This sample service is modeled after the ecumenical evening prayer services of the Taizé community in France.

Gathering
Prelude
Opening hymns: "Now on land and sea descending"
(HWB 655)
"There is a place of quiet rest" (HWB 5)
Psalm 16 with sung response: "Alleluia" (HWB 101)
(Divide the Psalm into stanzas and sing the Alleluia response after each one.)
Opening prayer
Silence

Hearing the Word
Hymn of light with candlelighting: "In thy holy place we bow" (HWB 2, verses 1,2)
Old Testament reading: Isaiah 38:9-20
Hymns: "Come, ye disconsolate" (HWB 497)
"O power of love" (HWB 593)
Gospel reading: Matthew 11:25-30
Silence
Hymn: "Cast thy burden upon the Lord" (HWB 586)

Responding in prayer

Prayers of intercession with sung response: "Kyrie"
  (HWB 152)

Lord's Prayer: "Our Father who art in heaven"
  (HWB 554)

Prayers around the cross with "Stay with me"
  (HWB 242)

(Participants may come to a cross or the Lord's table and kneel to offer silent prayers while the rest of the group sings.)

Sending

Blessing (HWB 772)

Closing hymn: "Go, my children" (HWB 433)

A Short Service of Prayer for Church Gatherings

A prayer for morning or evening (either at the beginning or end of the gathering)
Scripture reading
Silence
Intercessory prayer

Prayer at the Close of Day

Hymn(s) (HWB 652-658)
Opening Response

L: The Lord almighty grant us a quiet night and peace at the last.
P: Amen.
L: It is good to give thanks to the Lord,
P: To sing praise to your name, O Most High;
L: To herald your love in the morning,
P: Your truth at the close of day.

Confession

L: Let us confess our sin in the presence of God and one another.

Silence

P: I confess that I have sinned against you this day. Some of my sin I know—the thoughts and words and deeds of which I am ashamed—but some is known only to you. In the name of Jesus Christ I ask for-

giveness. Deliver and restore me that I
may rest in peace.

For Jesus' sake. Amen.

Psalm (one of the following is traditional: 4, 33, 34,
91, 134, 136)

Meditation

Hymn

Intercessory Prayer (free prayers and/or the following
may be used)

L: Lord, you have been our dwelling place
in all generations.

P: Dreams and seasons and nations pass
away, but you remain.

L: You are the guardian of time and eternity.

P: Now we offer the world you gave into
our care this morning back into your
hands; hear our prayer for it.

L: For all who tried to do good (silence after
each petition),
who willingly suffered evil,
who had to endure pain,
who sought the truth.

P: Lord, hear our prayer.

L: For all who are alone,
lost,
without peace,
dying.

P: Lord, hear our prayer.

L: For all who rule,
are oppressed,

lead the church,
have children in their care.

P: Lord, hear our prayer.

L: For ourselves that we might not deny
Christ,
that we might become more self-forgetting,
that we might not let the sun go down on
our wrath,
that we might live as if we believe the
world is in good hands.

P: Lord, hear our prayer, for Jesus' sake.
Amen.

Hymn (or a spoken or sung version of the following)

Lord, now you let your servant depart in
peace according to your word; for my eyes have
seen your salvation which you have prepared in
the presence of all peoples, a light for revelations
to the Gentiles and for glory to your people Israel.
(Lk. 2:29-32)

Benediction

L: Gracious Lord, we give you thanks for the
day, especially for the good we were per-
mitted to give and to receive. The day is
now past and we commit it to you. We
entrust to you the night. We rest in surety,
for you are our help and you neither
slumber nor sleep.

P: Amen.

L: Go in peace.

Resources for Prayer Services

Intercessions (see also HWB 718-722)

L: Keep us, O Lord, as the apple of your eye.
P: Hide us under the shadow of your wings.

L: For the peace of the whole world, we pray to you, Lord,
P: Lord, have mercy. (could be sung as in HWB 380)

L: For those who are weary, sleepless, and depressed, we pray to you, Lord,
P: Lord, have mercy.

L: For those who are hungry, sick, and frightened, we pray to you, Lord,
P: Lord, have mercy.

L: For rest and refreshment, we pray to you, Lord,
P: Lord, have mercy.

L: Guide us waking, O Lord, and guard us sleeping, that awake we may keep watch with Christ, and asleep rest in his peace.
P: Amen.

Evening Blessing

L: Bless to us, O God,

All: the moon that is above us,
      the friends who are around us,
      your image deep within us,
      the rest that is before us. Amen.[9]

If you wish to copy, contact G.I.A. Publications, phone 708 / 496-3800.

Opening Response for Evening Prayer

L: Come, Lord Jesus, you too were tired when day was done; you met your friends at evening time.

All: Come, Lord Jesus, meet us here.

L: Come, Lord Jesus. You kindled faith when lamps were low; you opened Scriptures, broke the bread and shed your light as darkness fell.

All: Come, Lord Jesus, meet us here.[10]

If you wish to copy, contact G.I.A. Publications, phone 708 / 496-3800.

Opening Response for Evening Prayer, Especially at Home

L: Come, Lord Jesus, be our guest, stay with us for day is ending. Bring to our house your poverty

All: For then we shall be rich.

L: Bring to our house your pain

All: That sharing it, we may also share your joy.

L: Bring to our house your understanding
of us

All: That we may be freed to learn more of you.

L: Bring to our house all those who hurry
toward you

All: That we may meet you as the Savior of all.

L: Bring to our house your Holy Spirit

All: That it may be a cradle of your love.[11]

*If you wish to copy, contact G.I.A. Publications,
phone 708 / 496-3800.*

Morning or Evening Blessing (see also the chapter
entitled **Blessing**)

Father God, we claim your Son's parting gift:
peace.

Not as the world gives, but only as he can give.

Set our hearts at rest; banish our fears.

Send the Advocate to dwell with us and go
with us until Jesus comes back,
the One who lives and reigns with you
and the Holy Spirit,
one God forever and ever. Amen.

Song of Praise for Daily Prayer (from Julian of Norwich)

God chose to be our mother in all things
and so made the foundation of his work
most humbly and most pure, in the
Virgin's womb.

God, the perfect wisdom of all,
arrayed himself in this humble place.

Christ came in our poor flesh
to share a mother's care.
Our mothers bear us for pain and for death;
our true mother, Jesus, bears us for joy
and for endless life.
Christ carried us within him in love and travail,
until the full time of his passion.
And when all was completed and he had
carried us so for joy,
still all this could not satisfy the power of
his wonderful love.
All that we owe is redeemed in truly loving God,
for the love of Christ works in us;
Christ is the one whom we love. Amen.[12]

Leonard Clock's Prayer for Morning
O Sovereign God, you are our creator and
provider.
Under your protection, we have been blessed
with another night of rest.
Teach us to ponder why you have created this
day,
so that we might spend it and all our days
mindfully, justly, and reverently.
May your name be honored in all that we do.
May your grace sustain us unto eternal life.
Let your good Spirit guide us and your angel
hallow our path.
O God, we ask this in the name of your
beloved Son. Amen.[13]

Hans de Ries' Prayer for Morning

> Merciful God, creator of all, we thank you for
> having kept us safe this night.
> You place the sun in the sky to give light on
> earth, dispelling the fear and darkness of
> night.
> Dispel now the fear and darkness in our souls
> through Jesus the Sun of righteousness.
> Quiet our conscience, remove the anxieties of
> our heart,
>> take from us the works of night and
>> clothe us with the light of your Word.
> Send your Holy Spirit to guide our work.
> Inspire our thoughts.
> Make our words gracious and our acts obedient.
> Keep us this day from sin, fear, and need
> and from the power of our enemies, both
> visible and invisible.
> Open the eyes of our heart to you
> through Christ, our guiding star
> and eternal light. Amen.[14]

Leonard Clock's Prayer for Evening

> Creator God, you have let the light of heaven
> shine on us
>> and granted us the day that is past
>> so that we might use it according to
>> your will.
> For this gracious gift we offer you thanks.

God of compassion, forgive us the things we
have left undone or done against your
will.
For the night before us, which you have
ordained for our rest,
defend us against the power of darkness.
Let us sleep in peace yet remain awake to
your presence.
O God, we pray for all the needs of your children,
their weaknesses and worries,
their suffering as your witnesses.
We pray for our persecutors.
Send workers to gather in your harvest.
Hear our petition for the rulers of all countries and cities.
Hear our cry for all who are troubled or fear-
ful, and cheer comfortless hearts.
Keep watch over us so that no one whom you
have created perishes
and everyone is brought to eternal
life.
This is our prayer to you through Jesus Christ
our Lord. Amen.[15]

Hans de Ries' Prayer for Evening

> Everlasting God, you have ordered the day
> for work and the night for rest.
>
> Keep us safe this night from the ruler of dark-
> ness and death.
>
> Grant that as our bodies rest, our souls may
> be awake to you.
>
> Set us free from thoughts that haunt us and
> failings that will not let us go.
>
> Grant our consciences peace.
>
> Forgive our sins, knowing and unknowing,
> through the merits of your Son.
>
> O Shepherd of Israel, who neither slumbers
> nor sleeps,
>
> > protect us under the shadow of your
> > wings from attacks by our enemies.
>
> When the last evening of our life comes,
>
> > and we are not to be awakened except by
> > the voice of an archangel,
> >
> > may we rest in you,
> >
> > committing our souls into your hands as
> > our bodies await a joyful resurrection at
> > the last day.
>
> Everlasting glory be to Christ,
>
> > who reigns with you and the Holy Spirit
> > from eternity to eternity. Amen.[16]

The Church Year and Lectionary[17]

Background

Early History

The church's first repeated celebration was the gathering of Christians on the first day of the week in commemoration of Jesus' resurrection. At an unknown but early date, Easter became not only a weekly but an annual celebration. The Christian calendar of annual celebrations has its origin in Judaism. The two best-known occasions which were carried over to Christianity from Judaism are Passover (our Easter) and Pentecost.

It was not until the end of the third century that the church began to commemorate other events out of Jesus' life annually. Then the church took upon itself the rhythms and responsibilities of historical time. It knew that it must sustain its members spiritually through the long interim between Christ's ascension and return. The church year became a bridge from the beginnings of the gospel to each age thereafter.

Mennonite Practice

At the time of the Reformation, sacred times were more often barriers to Christ rather than windows through which he was seen. The ritual imitations of events in the life of Jesus had often become a substitute for obedience to him. Pilgrim

Marpeck points this out with regards to Maundy Thursday. However, Marpeck does not conclude from this that Christians should not celebrate the church year but that it should be observed out of love.[18] It is evident, however, that under Reformed influence, the celebration of the church year receives little mention in the first two centuries of Mennonite history. References after the middle of the eighteenth century tell us that the Advent to Pentecost cycle was celebrated in some measure. Good Friday became the favored day for communion, and, in some circles, Pentecost became the day for baptisms. New Year's Eve and Day as well as Thanksgiving Day were widely celebrated, less so Eternity Sunday, the annual memorial for those who had died. In the twentieth century, Peace Sunday and family celebrations like Mothers' Day were added.

The Evolution of the Advent-Pentecost Cycle
Gradually Easter evolved into a short season of preparation culminating in the observance of Jesus' death and then his resurrection. From the diary of a Christian woman by the name of Egeria, we know how this feast was celebrated in Jerusalem in about A.D. 385. She describes a repetition of the events of that fateful week in Jesus' life. It began with a procession of palms and olives from Bethany into Jerusalem on the Sunday before Easter. On Thursday evening, the

Lord's Supper was celebrated. And on Good Friday, the three hours of Jesus' crucifixion were spent at the site of Calvary.

Historians dispute the way in which further evolution took place. It is clear, however, that the events in Jesus' life gradually gained a second level of meaning. Since Easter became a common date for baptism, the pre-Easter period had to be the time for preparation of candidates. The long and short of it is that after centuries of variable observances, most of the Western church fixed on a forty-day period prior to Easter in imitation of Jesus' forty days in the wilderness. For some centuries, this was observed primarily by the candidates for baptism. During the weeks before Easter, their confession and exorcism were observed. When infant baptism replaced believers' baptism, this penitential period of preparation called lent was enjoined on the whole church.

The next annual celebration to develop was Christmas. It was celebrated on January 6 in the East and December 25 in the West. Enormous variations of celebration surround this event. Again, a need was felt to prepare for the occasion. Therefore periods of from three to six weeks developed into what we call Advent. In many cases, Advent had two meanings. It was penitential in a sense, similar to that of Lent. But it was also expectant and joyful in that it used the certainty of Jesus' first coming as a promise of his second coming. This double character of Advent expressed the tension in which the church always lives. It needs to come to terms with history, yet it is restless for that kingdom beyond the fallenness of time.

January 6 was called Epiphany, the appearing. Two traditions have carried on through the centuries. One celebrates the arrival of the Magi. The second tradition, which liturgical scholarship accords theological and biblical precedence, focuses on Jesus' appearing not as a child but as an adult, when the Spirit descended upon him in his baptism.

Pentecost has a place in the Christian calendar because it was the day when the Jews in Jerusalem who had accepted Jesus as the Messiah received the Holy Spirit. Also called Whitsunday, Pentecost received a fixed place in the church's celebration in the early Middle Ages. We know this because it was the alternate date to Easter for baptism. Parallel to it came the celebration of Ascension Day ten days earlier. Pentecost is the climax of the church's salvation story. Almost subconsciously, the celebration of Pentecost kept alive the claim that the experience of Jesus is as possible to every subsequent generation as it was to those who met him in Galilee. Pentecost is the assertion that time is not a barrier to meeting Christ.

Lectionary

The use of Scripture to re-travel the events of Jesus' life inspired the development of lectionaries. A lectionary is simply a selection of readings to be used in sequence through the church year. Its intention is to present all aspects and books of Scripture and to highlight the great feasts and fasts of the church. Some Mennonites used a full lectionary in the eighteenth and nineteenth centuries. More often they have taken the themes of the seasons and used many of the texts found in the lectionaries but resisted prescribing them for mandatory usage.

The *Revised Common Lectionary* is an attempt to make the Roman Catholic three-year cycle and all those derived from it into a single coherent lectionary for all English-speaking Christians. The widespread acceptance of the *Revised Common Lectionary* is creating a commonality in the subject matter of Christian worship unheard of since before the Reformation.

Pastoral Considerations

Each season and its readings has its spiritual focus point. Let us take the example of Lent and examine the pastoral possibilities it opens up. The theme of Lent is repentance. In Jesus' ministry, as it moves toward the cross, Christians hear the call to deny themselves and suffer with Jesus. As was Jesus' ministry, so is our rehearsing of it a call to people who have never accepted Christ. Lent is a season in which evangelistic preaching is inescapable. The themes of Lent provide a biblical and spiritual framework for offering Christ. Lent is also a most meaningful time to encourage and deepen social-justice involvements. This dimension of mission is organic to the season because the suffering of Jesus is an act of solidarity with an oppressed human race.

Summary

Since we believe that God's self-disclosure comes to us through past events, we can recover the significance of those happenings by celebrating them in our present life. We know all year that Christ arose, but the commemorating of that event on a special day in a special way dramatically involves us in God's action. God's specific act of salvation at a definite time and place is experienced in worship to bring God's gift of the past into the present. We re-experience God's concrete acts of grace, which give ultimate meaning to life, and we respond to those past events out of the present moment.

The church year, with its focus on the weekly Lord's day and annual seasons and festivals, is the gradual outgrowth of the experiences and needs of Christians through the centuries. It provides a sense of historic depth to church life as it takes us back to the very life and teachings of

Jesus and assures a definitely Christian character to worship. It guards against the secular and social themes that focus very much on humanity's doings rather than on God's actions. In our acts of remembrance, God's work in history is made alive and refreshing to us in a vitality that can never be exhausted.

Baptism and Church Membership

Biblical Foundations

As an act of worship, baptism is firmly rooted in the Bible. In the Old Testament, the practice of ritual cleansing was commonly used to signify cleansing from sin and a desire to walk in the ways of God. This tradition formed the background for New Testament understanding and practice. John the Baptist invested baptism with important ethical significance and linked it with his proclamation of God's coming kingdom (Mt. 3:2, 8). John baptized Jesus as an ordination into God's mission and as a way to identify with his people. From the day of Pentecost, the early church practiced baptism as a symbol of entry into the Christian community (Acts 2:38, 41). It was closely connected with repentance and receiving the Holy Spirit.

The Bible presents baptism from numerous perspectives:

1. In baptism, we participate in Jesus' dying, being buried, and rising again. (Rom. 6:1-4)

2. In baptism, a believer becomes part of the witnessing, Christian community, the body of Christ. (1 Cor. 12:12, 13)

3. In baptism, we are born anew by water and Spirit. (Jn. 3:5)

4. In baptism, we are clothed with Christ in new garments, signifying a new creation so that

all human divisions are overcome. (Gal. 3:26-29; Eph. 4:5)

5. In baptism, we die to the ways of sin and are raised to a new life through our union with Christ. (Col. 2:9-15)

6. Baptism follows repentance and signifies an outpouring of the Holy Spirit. (Acts 2:38)

7. Baptism witnesses to the transforming power of the Holy Spirit in the believer's life. (Rom. 12:2)

8. Baptism is not a source or means of salvation. (2 Cor. 10:2)

Theological Foundations

Baptism celebrates God's act of redemption in the believer. It is an outward, visible sign of an inner, spiritual transformation made possible through the resurrected Christ. According to Article 11 of *Confession of Faith in a Mennonite Perspective*,[19] baptism signifies in public witness that the believer has received the gospel message, repented of sin, and earnestly desires to grow in faith and to follow Christ in daily life. Baptism is not in itself a salvific act, but witnesses to the saving activity of God in the believer.

Although the decision to follow Jesus and receive baptism is personal, it is not private. The living faith of the individual is expressed in the context of the community of faith for nurture, support, discipling, and mission. Baptism and church membership are inseparable. Baptism incorporates the believer into the community of kingdom citizens—the church—there to be accountable to and for others in all matters of faith and life.

Infants and children have no need of baptism since we believe them to be safe in God's grace until such time as they are fully accountable for their own actions. The Anabaptists said that Christ's atonement preserves children from judgment during the age of innocence. While there is constant temptation to seek baptism because one's peers or parents desire it, or because it is the expected thing at a certain age, these factors should not be allowed to hasten or postpone the decision. The request for baptism must arise out a personal confession of sin, the experience of grace and forgiveness (which sometimes comes in a crisis event, and sometimes gradually), and a commitment to Jesus Christ and to the congregation.

It is of utmost importance that the nature of God's initiative and our response be made clear to baptismal candidates. Becoming a Christian begins in the experience of grace. Through the work of Christ and the power of the Holy Spirit, God comes to us, freeing us from sin for obedience. Baptism is not the end but the beginning of a Christian's walk with God and the church. It is offered to sinners whose hearts are set on Christ. It is not reserved for people who have arrived at maturity of faith; it is intended for people who have come to Christ and want to live for him. By ourselves we cannot live a life of love. God works it in us through the indwelling of the Spirit, and through the biblically based counsel which sisters and brothers give one another. The obedience of faith is a lifelong process sustained by corporate and individual prayer, Bible study, and engagement with the world.

Historical Foundations

Baptism in the early church was the result of a mature commitment on the part of the recipient. Only believers aware of the import of their decision entered into it. Though there is some reference to the baptism of entire households (e.g., Acts 16:33) suggesting that young children may have received baptism, the overwhelming witness of the New Testament is that baptism was the result of mature commitments by believers conscious of their sin and having made commitments to Jesus Christ.

Baptism had three meanings for early Anabaptists:

1. Baptism of water which is an external representation of inner cleansing and baptism by the Spirit.

2. Baptism of the Spirit which empowers the daily life of the believer.

3. Baptism of blood, which is an expression of the willingness to suffer and endure great sacrifice for Christ.[20]

The Schleitheim Confession of 1527 states the following consensus on baptism: "Baptism shall be given to all those who have been taught repentance and the amendment of life and who believe truly that their sins are taken away through Christ, and to all those who desire to walk in the resurrection of Jesus Christ and be buried with him in death, so that they might rise with him; to all those who with such an understanding themselves desire and request it from us."[21]

Practical Considerations

Although the practice of baptism will vary among churches, a number of characteristics are essential. Baptism in the Mennonite church is properly constituted when:

- It is presided over by someone whom the congregation trusts and recognizes as a leader.
- It is conducted in the context of a gathered, believing community.
- It follows preparation through instruction in the Christian faith.
- It celebrates personal commitment and may include a testimony of the believer to Jesus Christ.
- It includes membership in the local congregation.
- It recognizes the mutual accountability of believers one to another.
- It uses water as a symbol of cleansing from sin, and burial and resurrection with Christ (physi-

cal form—i.e., pouring, sprinkling, or immersion—is secondary to theological content).

- The words spoken in this act of worship include confession of sin, a statement of commitment to Christ, the making of a covenant with God's people, and the trinitarian formula.
- It may include witnesses (elder/deacon, parents, mentors, spouse).
- It culminates in the Lord's Supper.

Preparation for baptism begins long before the actual day.[22] A number of guides to the initiation of new Christians are available with instructions and activities for the candidates and the congregation, up to and beyond the day of baptism. From the beginning, the testimony of each believer to the experience of grace and the desire to live out that grace in the company of the congregation has been integral to the practice of baptism. It is often grounded in Jesus' promise that everyone who acknowledges him before others, Jesus will acknowledge before God (Mt. 10:32-33). In more recent practice, the testimony is often given immediately prior to baptism. The earlier pattern was to have a congregational gathering a week or so beforehand so the congregation was able to ask questions and offer affirmation before the event. In some areas, two witnesses vouched for the faith of the candidate. A contemporary version of this custom is to give the role of witness to the candidate's mentor.

Ritual Actions

The full meaning of baptism comes to expression in a public service which includes preaching and culminates in the Lord's Supper. Except for extenuating circumstances, baptism belongs in the context of the congregation's normal worship. In baptism by pouring, the minister pours a quantity of water over the candidate's head by dipping with cupped hands from a bowl, or the deacon pours water from a pitcher into the cupped hands of the minister over the candidate's head. In baptism by sprinkling, the minister dips fingers into a bowl of water and sprinkles water on the candidate's head, one or three times. In baptism by immersion, the candidate is completely immersed in the water by the minister, usually by a single dip backwards. The deacon is present in the water to steady the candidate. Where immersion is the chosen mode of baptism but the church does not have a baptistry, alternate space arrangements need to be made which are free enough of distraction to foster the concentration and reverence on which a meaningful service depends. If the baptism is not held in the normal meeting place, it is still important that the whole congregation be present. Whatever the arrangements, it is important that the principal participants in the service be part of a rehearsal.

In order to affirm inclusive ways of describing God, some people advocate replacing the

Father, Son, Spirit formula with other biblically based terms for God. Even though the formulation in Matthew 28 is the most common warrant for baptism, the New Testament contains several other formulations. One of the services in this book offers alternate formulations. However, there is a conviction across the range of denominations that the historic trinitarian formula is irreplaceable.[23] Some go as far as to assert that baptism without this formula is invalid. This means, in the judgment of those who take this position, that someone baptized without the Father, Son, Spirit formula might not be received into another Christian community.

It has been common Mennonite practice to conclude the rite of baptism with a prayer of blessing, sometimes in the form of the invocation of the Holy Spirit, over each candidate. 1 Thessalonians 5:23-24 is a simple and widespread form of this blessing. The commissioning of new believers to ministry is an expansion of this action. A host of customs, some dating from the earliest Christian times, have survived in local settings. Where they are tied to the meaning of the event, such actions add to the service. For example, in some circles, the candidates are asked to dress in white as a sign of their having been clothed in the righteousness of Christ. In other circles, it is customary to choose a verse of Scripture for each candidate and to include it in

Hymns:
   "All who believe and are baptized" (HWB 436)
   "Count well the cost" (HWB 437)
   "I sing with exultation" (HWB 438)
   "I want Jesus to walk with me" (HWB 439)
   "I believe in you, Lord Jesus" (HWB 440)
   "I bind unto myself today" (HWB 441)
   "Christ be with me" (HWB 442)
   "We know that Christ is raised" (HWB 443)
   "Lord, I want to be a Christian" (HWB 444)
   "Come, Holy Spirit, Dove divine" (HWB 445)
   "Wade in the water" (HWB 446)
   "O Jesus, I have promised" (HWB 447)
   "Awake, awake, fling off the night" (HWB 448)

(See also HWB 6, 26-31, 81, 102, 111, 129, 143-153, 298-304, 307, 337, 338, 372, 395, 411, 524, 528, 535, 545, 597, 606)

Scripture passages:

Matthew 28:19-20	John 3	Romans 6:1-4
Mark 10:38	John 4:1	Galatians 3:2-7
Luke 12:50	Acts 2:38-39	1 John 5:7-8

Visual setting:

If the baptism will be by pouring or sprinkling, place the water to be used in a clear glass pitcher or bowl on a table at the front of the sanctuary where it will be visible to all. Consider creating a banner (quilted, painted, appliqued, etc.) that will be displayed at all baptisms. Colors appropriate for baptism include blue and silver (water), red (fire, blood of Christ), white (purity). A white candle may be carried in by the candidate.

the act of reception into the congregation. The act of reception is almost always concluded with a gesture of welcome such as the holy kiss and/or the right hand of fellowship.

THE RITE OF BAPTISM

Opening Remarks

Jesus said, "All authority in heaven and on earth has been given to me. Go therefore and make disciples of all nations, baptizing them in the name of the Father and of the Son and of the Holy Spirit, and teaching them to obey everything that I have commanded you. And remember, I am with you always, to the end of the age" (Mt. 28:18-20).

Because of Jesus' commandment and promise, we are here today. For this reason people make the covenant of baptism with God and the church. We are witnesses to their choice and companions to it.

Baptism is an act of God, of the church, and of the believer. In baptism, God gives us a good conscience and the seal of the Holy Spirit. Baptism enacts what God has done with us: made us dead to sin and alive to Christ. As an act of the church, baptism vouches for the faith of the believer and affirms the work of grace in her/his life. As an act of the individual, baptism enacts her/his surrender of the old self and the embrace of a new self, born in the image of Christ.

Questions

_____, do you renounce the evil powers of this world and turn to Jesus Christ as your savior? Do you put your trust in his grace and love and promise to obey him as your Lord?
Answer: I do.

Do you believe in God, the Father Almighty, maker of heaven and earth; in Jesus Christ, God's Son, our Lord; and in the Holy Spirit, the giver of life?
Answer: I do.

Do you accept the Word of God as guide and authority for your life?
Answer: I do.

Are you willing to give and receive counsel in the congregation?
Answer: I am.

Are you ready to participate in the mission of the church?
Answer: I am.

Personal address to each candidate (affirmation of gifts, expression of hope)

Baptism
On your confession of faith in Jesus Christ [*pour or sprinkle water, or immerse candidate see page 42*],

I baptize you with water in the name of the Father, the Son, and the Holy Spirit.

May God baptize you with the Holy Spirit from above. Amen.

All-powerful God, grant _____ the fullness of the Holy Spirit:
a clean heart, a right spirit, the joy of salvation.

Make her/him one in whom Christ is seen to live again.

Release the gifts you gave her/him in creation and redeemed in Christ.

_____, may the God of peace sanctify you wholly.

May your spirit and soul and body be kept sound and blameless until the coming of our Lord Jesus Christ.

The One who calls you is faithful and will do it. Amen.

Reception

_____, in the name of Christ and the church,

I give you my hand and bid you to rise and walk in newness of life
by the same power that raised Christ from the dead.

As long as you abide in his Word, you are Christ's disciple indeed
and shall be acknowledged as a brother/sister in the church.

[Giving of a baptismal verse to each candidate]

You have made the good confession of Jesus Christ
    and offered yourself to be our companion in obeying him.
May God bless you and make you a blessing in our midst.
The peace of Christ be with you. *(kiss of peace/right hand of fellowship)*

Congregational Response
We welcome you, _____,
    as a brother/sister in this congregation.
We join together as companions seeking the way of Christ,
        bearing one another's burdens,
        and sharing our gifts with the world.

OTHER BAPTISMAL QUESTIONS

(a)
Are you sorry for your sins?
Answer: I am.

Do you believe in God the Father, in Jesus Christ the Son, and in the Holy Spirit, the Giver of Life?
Answer: I do.

Do you promise, by God's grace, to follow Jesus, the Lamb, all the days of your life, ready to love your enemies and suffer wrong nonresistantly?
Answer: I do.

Do you accept the way of life set forth in our confession of faith?
Answer: I do.[24]

(b)
Let me ask you, in the hearing of this congregation, and in the name of the Lord and of his
church, for a public confession of your faith:

Do you, in the presence of God and this assembly,
solemnly renounce the Devil and all his works
and declare the Lord to be your God?
Answer: I do.

Do you confess the Lord Jesus Christ as your
Redeemer, trusting alone in the merits of his
death and resurrection for the forgiveness of your
sins, the sanctification of your fallen but now
redeemed nature, the resurrection of your body,
and everlasting salvation in heaven?
Answer: I do.

Do you solemnly pledge yourself to Christ and
his service, and will you by the power of the Holy
Spirit shun the ways of sin, seek communion with
God, and abide by his Word?
Answer: I will.

May God ratify this covenant and give you grace
to be steadfast in faith and love.[25]

(c) *(For situations in which very simple wording is required)*

Do you believe that Jesus loves you?
Answer: I do.

Do you believe that Jesus forgives you of all your sins?
Answer: I do.

Do you love Jesus and want to live by his teachings?
Answer: I do.

Do you want to be a member of this church?
Answer: I do.

OTHER BAPTISMAL FORMS

(a)
Upon your confession of faith, I baptize you with water in the name of God the Creator, Redeemer, and Sustainer. May God baptize you with the Holy Spirit.

(b)
Upon your confession of faith, I baptize you in the name of God, in the name of Christ Jesus, and in the name of the Holy Spirit, the holy Trinity.

OTHER PRAYERS OF BLESSING
CONCLUDING BAPTISM

(a)

Almighty God,
> we give you thanks that in the beginning
> your Spirit moved upon the face of the waters
> and you said, "Let there be light."

We give you thanks that you led your people
> through the waters of the Red Sea,
>> out of slavery, and into the freedom of the
>> Promised Land.

We give you thanks for your Son, Jesus Christ,
> who was baptized in the river Jordan.

We thank you that he passed through the deep
> water of death on the cross
> and was raised to life in triumph.

Send us your Holy Spirit,
> that this baptism may manifest for your servants
> their union with Christ in his death and resurrection,
> and that, as Christ was raised from death
>> through the glory of the Father, they also
>> might live new lives.

Send your Holy Spirit anew upon them
> that they may be brought into the fellowship
>> of the body of Christ
> and may grow in Christ's likeness.

Hear us, for his sake. Amen.[26]

(b)

O God, creator of all things visible and invisible,
 for the gift of _____'s life and for your
 saving presence in it,
 we give you thanks.
 Be present in the trials and joys of his/her life
 that he/she may always trust your love.
O Jesus, perfect image of God and perfect image
 of humanity,
 for your life of faithfulness we give thanks.
 Guide _____ so that he/she may always
  trust your grace.
O Holy Spirit, sustainer and teacher,
 for your energy moving in and around
 _____, we give thanks.
 Strengthen him/her so that he/she may
  always trust your promises. Amen.[27]

(c)

Following an ancient practice of the church, we are now to commission those who have been baptized to ministry as priests and servants of Jesus Christ. Let us as members of this congregation join with them and renew our commitment to the servant ministry of Christ.

You are a chosen race, a royal priesthood, a holy nation, God's own people, in order that you may proclaim the mighty acts of the one who called you out of darkness into light. (1 Pet. 2:9)

(Those who have been baptized kneel before the table, while the minister lays hands on them and prays freely or as follows:)

Eternal God, cause your Spirit to come upon these your servants to confirm them in ministry for the church and the world. May they be so filled with your love that as they live in the world, the world may know the love of Christ. Amen.

(The newly commissioned ones stand, and the minister says:)

You are no longer strangers and aliens, but you are members of the household of God. On behalf of this congregation, I welcome you. May the peace of God go with you always. Amen.[28]

OTHER WORDS OF RECEPTION

(a)
As brothers and sisters in the body of Christ and
    members of this congregation,
      we welcome you, _____, as a
    brother/sister into Christ's church.
We witness to the work of the Holy Spirit who
    has led you to Jesus as Savior
    and to God as the source of your life.
We promise to encourage you in faith,
    to rejoice with you in joy,
    to support you in suffering,
    to guide you in confusion,
    to listen to the word God speaks in you,

and to call out the gifts the Holy Spirit is
creating in you.
We thank God for your presence in the body of
Christ,
and we ask God's blessing on you all the days
of your life.[29]

(b)
Arise, shine, for your light has come
and the glory of the Lord is upon you.
Stand up in the name of the Lord Jesus Christ;
be steadfast in the path he has set you upon.
I give you the hand of fellowship:
welcome into the church of Jesus Christ.

(c)
In the name of Christ and the church, I now
extend to you the right hand of fellowship
and welcome you, _____, as a
brother/sister into the church of Christ.

MEMBERSHIP TRANSFER

As new people are attracted to the congregation's
life of worship, fellowship, and service, it is
appropriate to provide opportunities for their formal reception as members. Most Mennonite congregations will receive members from other
Mennonite congregations and Christian denominations by letter of transfer or upon a reaffirmation of their faith commitment.

It is important to allow people a free choice concerning membership transfer. At the same time, the congregation can provide an invitational context for this to occur. Such options as newcomers' classes, faith refresher courses, invitations through the bulletin, and direct personal encouragement by church members and the pastor can be very helpful.

When a person is ready to join the congregation, the following steps may be considered as part of the transfer process:

1. The person requesting transfer arranges for a letter of transfer and/or recommendation from the previous place of worship.

2. The receiving congregation may request a clear and public re-affirmation of faith.

3. The receiving pastor shares names of prospective members with the congregation and its leadership.

4. Persons baptized as children or infants in another Christian tradition should be invited to baptism on the basis of present faith, especially where infant baptism was not followed with a process which nurtured the individual into mature faith. However, insistence on a believer's baptism should not be allowed to obscure the individual's desire to seek meaningful membership. More emphasis should be placed on the confession and life witness of the believer and the denomination to which the believer belonged than on the act of baptism itself.

COVENANT RENEWAL

There are times when church membership loses its meaning. Members may become inactive and withdraw their practical participation from the congregation. Sometimes the believer's original commitment lacked depth; at other times there has been serious hurt resulting in alienation; sometimes the church has failed in its attempt to be redemptive in discipling its members. If we have made sensitive attempts to heed people's hurts, needs, and concerns, we should respect their choice to discontinue their association with the church and release them graciously.

For those who continue their membership and participation, it is desirable to provide periodic opportunities for celebration and renewal of the membership covenant. This could be done in several ways: (1) through a covenant-renewal service including a reaffirmation of baptismal vows; (2) by making one communion service per year a time to share, celebrate, and renew commitments; or (3) using a regular worship service to focus on the meaning of Christian discipleship in the context of church membership.

The Lord's Supper

Biblical Foundations

The primal act of the Christian church is its gathering to eat bread and drink wine in memory of Jesus. This ritual meal had its origin in Jewish tradition as a re-enactment of the Exodus from Egyptian bondage. The Christian breaking of bread recalls Jesus' meals with seekers and friends before and after his resurrection (Mk. 2:18-22, 6:30-44; Lk. 24:13-35; Jn. 21:9-14) and, supremely, the Passover supper at which Jesus inaugurated a new covenant in his death (Mk. 14:12-25). In the supper at Emmaus, we have an early description of the meaning of such encounters: He had been made known to them in the breaking of the bread (Lk. 24:35). After Jesus' ascension, the early Christians believed that the breaking of bread in his name was a communion of his body and blood (1 Cor. 10:16).

Historical Background

Throughout Christian history, the church has sought to grasp the paradox that God's transcendent reality can be symbolized by earthbound elements. The beloved communion hymn "Deck thyself with joy" says it well: "Come, for now the King most holy stoops to thee in likeness lowly." From a free church vantage point, the long historical debates concerning the eucharist have focused

too much on bread and wine as objects and too little on the church as the body of Christ in the
world. As Mennonites understand it, the transformation that occurs in communion is that of people
and not objects. In the Middle Ages, the elements
were held to be so holy that people dreaded to
take communion. As a consequence, even though
there was a consecration in each mass, people
took communion only once or twice a year.

The Reformation claimed that grace was
given in sacraments only to faith: bread and wine
are signs of Christ's presence by the power of the
Spirit. When received in faith and love by the
gathered community, bread and wine become a
communion of Christ's body and blood. In the
simplest possible terms, this was the teaching of
most of the Protestant Reformers, including most
of the Anabaptists. Some of the Reformers sought
to restore frequent communion but were unable
to do so consistently because of the persistence of
the medieval dread of unworthy communion. In
addition, Anabaptists emphasized seeking peace
with fellow church members as a precondition for
the breaking of bread as well as communing only
when the whole congregation is gathered. During
times of persecution, this was seldom possible.
Thus, a tendency toward perfectionism and persecution reinforced the existing practice of infrequent communion. There was, however, frequent
communion in some early Anabaptist circles. For

example, the Schleitheim Confession recommends breaking bread as often as the church gathers. This practice is commended by *Confession of Faith in a Mennonite Perspective* on page 52.

From the beginning of the seventeenth to the beginning of the twentieth century in our two streams of Mennonitism, there was an almost universal pattern for communion. The service was held two or three times a year, following either the seasons (spring and fall) or the church year (Good Friday, Pentecost, and Eternity Sunday or First Advent). It consisted of a preparatory service or counsel meeting held either a week or a day before the breaking of bread. The service of the bread and cup was almost always completed by footwashing. The problems of legalism and gracelessness led to changes in this pattern, in which one or both of the preparatory services and footwashing were dropped. We do well to adapt this pattern according to pastoral need but also to remember the threefold action as our norm. In some circles, the practice developed of concluding communion with an act of thanksgiving in the form of testimonies or prayers from the congregation and/or the reading of a psalm (most often Psalm 103).

With the separation of the free churches from traditional liturgical life after the Reformation and under the influence of a scientific worldview in the nineteenth century, the Lord's Supper came more and more to be seen as a rational act of human memory, almost a "real absence" of Christ. The advent of ecumenical biblical scholarship, a richer theology of grace, and the recovery of an appreciation for the nonrational dimensions of human experience are leading to a fuller theology and practice of communion in all churches.[30]

Theological Foundations

Rituals condense vast realities into simple gestures. The Lord's Supper concentrates the saving work of Christ into a moment and an action. We gather around bread and wine in the faith that Christ is both our host and our food (Zwingli). The eucharist is not a sacred object in which Christ is contained; it is a sacred event. When the church gathers in faith and love, open to the power of the Spirit, Christ is made present in the sharing of bread and wine.

Just as he did in his earthly ministry, Jesus comes now and invites us to receive him; the initiative is his, but the response is ours. Thus, the breaking of bread has as much to do with our presence as with his. We prepare ourselves to receive Christ by turning our back on other loyalties and by seeking peace with all (Mt. 5:23-24). This process begins in conversion and baptism but continues throughout our lives: we go our own way and then return. The Lord's Supper condenses into a gesture this ongoing return to Christ and to our sisters and brothers.

What constitutes a true celebration of the Lord's Supper in a Mennonite understanding of the Gospel? Communion happens when:

1. A community of baptized believers gathers in faith and love. Communion is the resetting of the bones of the body of Christ, the remaking of our relationship with him and one another.[31] Because it is inherently communal, every celebration, even under special circumstances, is an extension of the congregation (e.g., at a sick bed or on a retreat). To gather in faith and love involves taking stock of oneself and one's relationships and regrounding them in Christ. Therefore, some act of self-examination is called for. When communion was celebrated only twice a year, a day was set aside to restore unity in the congregation. In some circles, communion was postponed when reconciliation could not be found. We now judge that our ancestors emphasized holiness of life to the point of legalism and underemphasized grace as the source of holiness. The fear of falling short of God's commandments was one reason for infrequent communion. Many congregations now celebrate communion more frequently, and so the burden of restoring unity does not fall only on two occasions. Pastoral judgment is necessary to determine the balance between a call to self-examination and assurance of grace in setting the tone for the service.

2. It is presided over by someone whom the congregation trusts as a true shepherd of Christ, usually but not necessarily ordained.

3. Scripture reading and proclamation set forth the saving work of Christ.

4. The words of institution are spoken. They tie us to the original event; they are a warrant from Jesus himself for what we are about to do; and they are the words we have in common with every other community which breaks bread in Jesus' name.

5. Prayer is made, thanking God for the broken body and shed blood and their signs of bread and wine, and asking for the Spirit to make Christ known in the breaking of bread. In Jewish as well as Christian sacred meals, God was blessed for God's saving work. Following the narratives of the Last Supper, free churches have interpreted this blessing to be simple prayers of remembrance and thanks for Jesus' life given for us (Mt. 26:26-29 and parallels). Some traditional Mennonite prayers also pray for the work of the Spirit in our midst (e.g., HWB 787). With other denominations, we are realizing more deeply that it is the work of the Spirit which makes our gathering a communion of the body and blood of the Lord.[32]

Pastoral Considerations

We are rightly concerned to receive Christ and our brothers and sisters worthily, but we should be careful not to conclude that, therefore, the whole action and outcome of communion depends on us. What constitutes the Lord's Supper is the presence of Christ; our preparation, our reverence, our obedience are the response. Yet we often think that if there is not a certain intensity of piety, nothing will happen. Unless we believe that Christ is the host, we have no adequate basis for frequent communion: the strain of having to come in a perfect commitment of faith and life every time will be too much for people; or they will trivialize the Lord's Supper and simply make it another fellowship hour.

It was mentioned earlier that our practice of infrequent communion is an inheritance from the Middle Ages. Recast into Anabaptist terms, the awe in which the Lord's Supper was held helped to make clear that it is an event in which relationships are restored. The reverence with which most traditional Mennonites come to the Lord's Supper is profound and should not be lost. At the same time, the emphasis on relationships and the later reduction of the eucharist to an act of human remembering has made the occasion burdensomely human centered. According to Article 12 of the *Confession of Faith*, frequent communion makes theological and pastoral sense when it balances the emphasis on Christ as the host and the giver with that of the unity of the church.

Many dimensions of salvation come to expression in the Lord's Supper. Some of them are identified by the names we use: Lord's Supper (remembrance of the original occasion), Communion (encounter), Eucharist (thanksgiving), Breaking of Bread (fellowship), and Banquet (a foretaste of the kingdom). The breaking of the bread and pouring of the cup represent the broken body and shed blood of Christ, his perfect and sufficient sacrifice, his vicarious suffering on behalf of the whole world. This reality is the heart of the gospel and of the Holy Supper. But there is more. We not only memorialize the slain Christ but also worship the risen Christ. We gather not only to repent of our broken relationships but also to celebrate their restoration. We not only contend with our mortality but also anticipate eternal life and the messianic banquet. Something of these realities should be present every time we break bread, yet it is also appropriate to highlight one of them according to the church calendar and the needs of the congregation.

Increasingly, a need is expressed for assurance of forgiveness after the confession of sin. Of course, this need is addressed in the giving of pastoral care. But it is also fitting to do so to conclude the preparation for communion. Seen from our understanding of the church, it seems right for the presider to be included in the declaration (e.g., "If *we* confess...," 1 Jn. 1:9, or "In the name of Jesus Christ, I declare that *we* are forgiven, loved, and free").

The question of who is invited to the table has become an urgent one. Open communion arose because of the gracelessness of much church life and, consequently, of many communion services. We now welcome all baptized Christians to the table in an act of ecumenical hospitality.[33] Can this hospitality be extended to unbaptized believers?

Traditionally, Mennonites have claimed that it is the covenant established with Christ and the church in conversion and baptism which admits us to the fellowship of the table. This is a sound norm, if we realize that people come to it in different ways. In his table fellowship, Jesus set no conditions for participation, but the encounter led to a decision for or against him. There is room at the Lord's Table for new believers who long to meet Christ and their sisters and brothers in the breaking of bread. But the encounter implies a decision: will they covenant with Christ and the church, and will they accept baptism, the sign of that covenant? Thus, the participation of unbaptized believers at communion is always preparatory, always anticipating baptism.

Because they have come to represent the body and blood of Christ, bread and wine remaining after the service should be reverently disposed of—either consumed after the service or at a meal or deposited on the ground in a natural setting.

Practical Considerations
The Order of Service
The norm for the Lord's Supper is the Sunday service with Scripture reading and preaching cul-

minating in the eucharist. The singing of hymns about the work of Christ and the fellowship of the church can accompany each step of the service. The act of preparation (self-examination, reconciliation with others) can come at a preparatory service, at the beginning of the service, or immediately before the communion. Being reconciled to God can be meaningfully climaxed by a gesture of reconciliation among the congregants, such as the passing of the peace.

An invitation to the Lord's Table follows the congregational prayer. The presider offers a general communion prayer, recalling the mighty works of God, climaxing in the saving death of Jesus, and praying for the Holy Spirit to make the breaking of bread a communion of the body of Christ. Thereafter the words of institution are read, either all at once or separately, attached to the prayers of thanks for the bread and the cup.

In settings where people go forward to receive, it is possible to combine the prayers of thanks for the bread and the cup. They are arranged so that the words of institution and prayers may be read together for both bread and wine. One historical practice has been for the congregation to receive communion in the rows, but there are precedents for communicants to come forward, either to receive individually or collectively around the table. In the rows, either the minister distributes one or both of the elements, saying lines from the words of institution, or deacons pass them along the pews. When individuals come forward, the same words may be used. When the whole congregation or part of it comes forward, people may pass the elements among themselves with the words of institution or other fitting words. It is appropriate for the minister to commune last. In some congregations, participants give the person to whom they pass the elements a silent nod of affirmation, inviting him or her to join in. Some congregations have begun dipping the bread into the wine (intinction). On the one hand, some people believe that intinction is more hygienic. On the other hand, it deletes the act of drinking from the eucharistic action. When there is footwashing, people go to the basins two at a time and wash each other's feet or they go as a group who wash each other's feet sequentially. One person kneels before the other, cupping water over the feet and drying them with a towel. Then the other reciprocates, and they greet each other with the holy kiss or embrace and a word of blessing. A time of silence or hymn singing may follow, or a prayer such as HWB 783 may be used. Communion concludes with the post-communion prayer or another act of thanksgiving and sending.

Presider's Role
It is common in Mennonite circles for more than one person to play a role in serving the Lord's

Supper. At the same time, one person should be the presider who invites people to participate and draws the event to a close. The other leaders and the congregation need to know that someone is overseeing the service. Traditionally, the bishop or leading minister served as host, and other ministers and deacons assisted with prayers, distribution, and footwashing. The underlying principle, which is applicable also to our pluralistic leadership patterns today, is that presiding at the Lord's Table belongs to those who lead and serve the congregation.

It is important that clear and crisp directions be given so people will know what is expected of them. This is best done at the time of the words of invitation, which allows the service to flow without interruption.

Intimacy

Communion is at the same time an intimate and a public event. It is intimate because in this feast, we meet Christ as he really is (the incarnation of grace) and our brothers and sisters as they really are (given a relationship with Christ and one another by grace). The hymn says it well, "Here, O my Lord, I see thee face to face. Here would I touch and handle things unseen." Though profoundly personal, the breaking of bread is a public event in that all who belong to Christ are invited; it is not a private event in which only people with particular attachments to one another gather.

Footwashing is an inevitably intimate encounter. Because of that, it is hard to enter into it often. But in a setting of warmth and serenity, it is a gesture of love which words stammer to express (see HWB 783). It prepares for or completes the breaking of bread most effectively in Holy Week, when we re-enter the events of Jesus' passion, or on occasions when the covenanting aspect of communion is given prominence.

Hymns:
"Jesus took a towel" (HWB 449)
"Here in our upper room" (HWB 450)
"Ubi caritas et amor" (HWB 452)
"Let us break bread together" (HWB 453)
"Seed, scattered and sown" (HWB 454)
"Bread of life" (HWB 455)
"I come with joy to meet my Lord" (HWB 459)
"Let the hungry come to me" (HWB 464)
"Here, O my Lord, I see thee" (HWB 465)
"Eat this bread" (HWB 471)
"I am the Bread of life" (HWB 472)
"This is the feast of victory" (HWB 476)
"Sent forth by God's blessing" (HWB 478)
(See also HWB 1, 6, 128-153, 235, 250, 252, 259, 260, 267, 305-311, 411, 449-478, 493, 514, 516, 522, 524)

Scripture passages:
Psalm 34:1-8   John 6:35-40, 47-51
Jeremiah 31:31-34   1 Corinthians 10:16
Isaiah 25:6-10   1 Corinthians 11:23b-26
Luke 22:14-20, 28-30   Revelation 19:6-9a
Luke 24:13-35

Visual setting:
Consider creating a banner (quilted, painted, appliqued, etc.) that will be displayed when the congregation celebrates communion. In some churches, part of the tradition is that the same kind of bread is always used for communion. The layers of meaning in communion can be expanded by choosing different kinds of bread for different themes. For example, a hearty whole-wheat loaf may be appropriate during Holy Week. For Easter morning, a braided loaf with a rich egg dough would be festive. On World Communion Sunday, use a variety of breads to represent the worldwide fellowship of the church: pita, bagels, rye bread, tortillas, zwieback, sourdough, cornbread, etc. Consider also varying the manner of distribution: coming forward, sitting in rows, standing in a circle, sitting at the table, etc.

The Service of Word and Table on the Lord's Day

FORM 1

Gathering in silence or with music

Hymn(s)

If there has not been a previous act of preparation, it may occur now or at the beginning of communion. One such act of preparation (to be read in unison) follows:

Before I take the body of the Lord, before I share his life in bread and wine, I recognize the sorry things within: these I lay down.

Silent prayer

The words of hope I often failed to give, the prayers of kindness buried in my pride, the signs of care I argued out of sight: these I lay down.

Silent prayer

The narrowness of vision and of mind, the need for other folk to serve my will, and every word and silence meant to hurt: these I lay down.

Silent prayer

Of those around in whom I meet my Lord, I ask their pardon and I grant them mine, that every contradiction to Christ's peace might be laid down.

Silent prayer

Lord Jesus Christ, companion at this feast, I empty now my heart and stretch my hands, and ask to meet you here in bread and wine which you lay down. Amen.[34] *If you wish to copy, contact G.I.A. Publications, phone 708 / 496-3800.*

Christ's Peace (either here or at the beginning of communion)

Hear the words of the Lord Jesus: "Peace I leave with you; my peace I give to you. I do not give to you as the world gives. Do not let your hearts be troubled, and do not let them be afraid" (Jn. 14:27). Let us offer one another the peace of Christ. *People turn to one another and with a handshake or embrace, wish each other Christ's peace. This is not a time for extended conversation but a mutual act of acceptance based on Christ's acceptance of us (Rom. 15:7). The simple line "I wish you the peace of Christ" suffices. Or one person may say, "The peace of Christ be with you," and the other responds, "And also with you."*

Scripture readings

Sermon

Congregational prayer (which should include prayer for the church in every place; for the peace of the world; for those in positions of public trust; for those in sickness, poverty, danger, sorrow, and suffering; and for ourselves)

Offertory

Invitation

Brothers and sisters in Christ,
    it is right that we call to mind the
    meaning of this Supper.
It is a remembrance of the sacrifice of Christ
    for the sin of the world;
    an encounter with the risen Lord;
    a feeding on him in faith;
    a communion with one another in his body,
    the church;
    and an anticipation of the day when he will
    come again.
It is the Lord's Table, and all who are baptized are
    invited to it.
Therefore, let us come to the Lord's Table in faith,
    knowing our weakness,
    renouncing our sin,
    trusting in Christ,
    seeking his grace.[35]

The act of preparation may follow here.

[Anointing may follow here, immediately after receiving communion, or at the end of the service. See the anointing section under **Healing and Lament**.*]*

Hymn

Communion Prayer and Lord's Prayer
O God of perfect love,
    through Jesus, your Son, we have come to
    know you.

In the company of the whole communion of saints,
 we come before you in this remembrance of
 Jesus' death
 with gratitude for your great redemption.

We praise you in the congregation of those you
 have called to be your companions and servants.

We thank you that you forgive those who are
 repentant.

You did not spare your only and beloved Son but
 offered him up to a bitter death.

You sent us a friend of sinners and gave us a new
 covenant.

With his stripes we are healed.

O God of bountiful grace,
 gratitude fills our hearts as we come to the
 Lord's Table.

Let it be a sign to us that you are a God who forgives us gladly and accepts us graciously.

Let this bread and cup show forth Christ's work
 of redemption.

In this Holy Supper, make us one with him
 that we might be steadfast in following him.

Send your Spirit to sanctify our hearts
 so that we might praise our Redeemer
 and taste his presence now and evermore.

Let the bread we break and the cup we drink be a
 communion of the body and blood of Christ.

Hear us for his sake, in whose name we pray,

Our Father who art in heaven,
Hallowed be thy name.
Thy kingdom come.
Thy will be done on earth,
As it is in heaven.
Give us this day our daily bread.
And forgive us our sins,
As we forgive those who sin against us.
And lead us not into temptation,
But deliver us from evil:
For thine is the kingdom, and the power, and
the glory, forever. Amen.[36]

*Communion (during the words of institution, the
bread and wine may be held aloft; the prayers of thanks
may be spontaneous)*

Words of institution for the bread:
For I received from the Lord what I also handed
on to you,
that the Lord Jesus on the night when he
was betrayed took a loaf of bread,
and when he had given thanks, he broke it
and said, "This is my body that is for you.
Do this in remembrance of me."

Prayer of thanks for the bread:
Bless, O Christ, the bread that we break.
Make it the bread of our holy communion with
you.

Open our eyes that we might see you by faith,
    on the cross, our reconciliation with God.
May your immeasurable act of generosity draw
    us to love you and serve you always. Amen.

At the beginning of the distribution of the bread:
Eat, beloved, eat the Lord's Bread.

Words of institution for the cup:
In the same way he took the cup also after
    supper, saying,
        "This cup is the new covenant in my blood.
        Do this as often as you drink it in
        remembrance of me."
For as often as you eat this bread and drink the cup,
    you proclaim the Lord's death until he comes.

Prayer of thanks for the cup:
O Lamb of God, you shed your blood on the cross
    for us.
Praised be your holy name for your grace and
    love.
Bless this cup, O Lord.
Make it the communion of your blood,
    so we may find rest for our souls and joy for
    our journey. Amen.

At the beginning of the distribution of the cup:
Drink, beloved, drink the Lord's Cup.[37]

At this time or during the footwashing, extemporaneous prayers, testimonies, and hymn singing may follow.

Footwashing
Read John 13 (all or part of verses 1-17) and give a short commentary on its meaning, or pray HWB 782.

When he washed his disciples' feet, Jesus set an example for us to follow.

In those days, only servants stooped before their masters to wash their feet.

Jesus, the Lord and Teacher, emptied himself, taking the form of a slave.

In kneeling before one another, we show our readiness to serve sister and brother, neighbor and enemy.

As we return to the tasks of daily life, may we remember the posture we have taken here.

Footwashing is also a sign of our need for cleansing of all that keeps us from a servant's stance.

In his humble act, Jesus purified the disciples of pride and concern for status.

As we allow another, in Christ's stead, to wash our feet, we open ourselves to that cleansing.

Come and renew the covenant of servanthood!

During the washing, silence may be kept or hymns may be sung.

To conclude, read John 13:17 or pray HWB 783.

Post-communion prayer
Blessed are you, O God.
You set aside this bread and cup as signs of your
    Son's broken body and shed blood,
    [this basin as a sign of his servanthood].
Through them you have made us partakers of
    Christ and of one another.
As we go forth,
            give us grace to count others better than
            ourselves,
            to love our enemies, and to seek peace.
Send the Spirit of Truth to keep alive in us what
    Jesus taught and did,
            in whose name we pray. Amen.

Hymn
Dismissal in silence or with music

If communion is celebrated in a separate service following the principal service of the Lord's
Day, the sermon appropriately focuses on the
work of Christ, often based on texts like Isaiah 53
and Luke 22. The congregational prayer and
other aspects of a regular service are usually
omitted in order to concentrate on fellowship
with Christ and one another. If the service takes
the form of a love feast, Form 2 is recommended.

If communion is shared with the sick or home-
bound, it is desirable that this be done as an extension of the congregational service. The above service may be abbreviated as appropriate or the fol-

lowing order may be used. It is best that the communion prayer not be repeated to make clear that the second service is an extension of the first service.

COMMUNION UNDER SPECIAL CIRCUMSTANCES

(Hymn)
Gathering Prayer
Scripture and word of commentary
Invitation
Act of self-examination/anointing/lifting up of needs
Assurance of pardon
Christ's peace
Words of institution

Prayer (HWB 788)
Blessed are you, God of heaven and earth.
In mercy for our fallen world you gave your
   only Son,
         that all those who believe in him should
         not perish but have eternal life.
We give thanks to you for the salvation
         you have prepared for us through Jesus
         Christ.
Send now your Holy Spirit into our hearts,
         that we may receive our Lord with a living
         faith as he comes to us in his holy supper.[38]
   (may be concluded with the Lord's Prayer)

Distribution
Post-communion prayer
(Hymn)

FORM 2

(adaptation of a seventeenth-century service by
Hans de Ries, especially suited for a love feast
and/or fellowship meal)

Introduction
After the Paschal lamb had been eaten, Jesus took
    ordinary bread.
Then he said a blessing over the bread,
        not only for that bread in that time but to the
        end of the world.
This bread is holy in its purpose—it has become a
    sign of Christ.
Therefore, we come to the feast with heartfelt
    thanks.
Because we easily forget what is out of sight,
        the Lord gives us this visible sign so that we
        might always think of him.
There could be no figure which more nearly
    represents the mystery at hand
        than the parable of bread and wine for the
        body and blood of Christ.
For as bread feeds and strengthens the outer person,
    so also does the body of Christ feed us
    inwardly in faith.
The bread is broken just as his body was also broken.
In the same way the wine gladdens the heart and
    quenches thirst;
        the blood of Christ does the same.

Silent prayer of thanks

A fellowship meal and/or Scripture, preaching, and prayer may follow here. Especially at a fellowship meal the following texts are suggested: Genesis 18:1-14; Psalm 33; 1 Corinthians 12.

Communion

What a magnificent Supper this is!
This is not ordinary eating and drinking. O no!
For the dinner host is God;
> the one who presides is Christ;
> all believers are his guests,
> and the food is the power of the flesh and spilled blood of Jesus.

Who is suitable to partake?
> Those who have a hearty faith in the love of God and the Word.
> Those who are filled with remorse for
>> their sins
>>> and trust in their hearts that God forgives sinners for Christ's sake.
> Those who live in purity for God, heeding the voice of our Shepherd, Jesus Christ.

Silence

Prayer

Therefore let there be no sorrow, no hesitance
> about coming to the table of the Lord,
>> for there we receive the forgiveness of our sins and the promise of eternal life.

Before we enter the wedding feast, let us call on
the name of the Lord.

O most gracious God, Father of our Lord Jesus
Christ,
> we are gathered here to keep your feast,
> to remember the death of our Savior,
> Jesus Christ.

We are not as we ought to be.
> We suffer sin.
> We transgress your Divine Majesty in
> thought, word, and deed.
> We know that you have good reasons not
> to feed us with your Son's body and blood.
> We cry out, Forgive us!

Draw our hearts to you that we may seek that
heavenly bread which feeds our souls in
eternal life. Amen.

Words of institution (1 Cor. 11:23-26)

For I received from the Lord what I also handed
on to you,
> that the Lord Jesus on the night when he
> was betrayed took a loaf of bread,
> and when he had given thanks,
> he broke it and said,
> "This is my body that is for you.
> Do this in remembrance of me."

In the same way he took the cup also, after
supper, saying,

"This cup is the new covenant in my blood. Do this, as often as you drink it, in remembrance of me."

For as often as you eat this bread and drink the cup, you proclaim the Lord's death until he comes.

For the bread:

The bread that we break, is it not a communion of the body of Christ?

We, though many, are one body since we are all participants in one bread.

As the bread is milled from many grains

> and is then one so that we can no longer distinguish the fat from the lean,

> just so we are one in Christ.

Jesus took the bread and first gave thanks before he broke it.

Therefore, let us in this too follow Christ and give thanks, saying:

> O eternal, friendly God, your Son gave his life for us sinners on the cross

>> and left us this Supper to his remembrance.

> Bless this bread for us this day through your Divine Power

>> so that it may provide for us a true sacrament

>> and be a true sign of your Son's body.

> By the partaking of this bread, grant us a higher,

namely a heavenly bread, Jesus Christ, who feeds our souls now and in eternal life. Amen.

Distribution
Take, eat, this is my body which is broken for you.

For the cup:
In this cup, grapes are now mixed with one another.
They, being joined together, quench thirst and give joy.
The cup of thanksgiving with which we give thanks, is it not the communion of the blood of Christ?
Since the Lord first blessed it, let us also bless it.

Compassionate God, you do not wish our death as sinners but that we turn around and live.
This cup presents before our eyes the outpouring of Christ's precious blood.
Bless it so that we might taste your salvation, and one day drink the new wine in the Father's kingdom. Amen.

Distribution
Drink all of it, this is my blood of the New Testament
which is poured out for many unto the forgiveness of sins.

After the Distribution
O taste and see that the Lord is good.
Footwashing may follow (see basic form).

Thanksgiving
Bless the Lord, O my soul,
     and all that is within me,
     bless his holy name.
Bless the Lord, O my soul,
     and do not forget all his benefits—
who forgives all your iniquity,
     who heals all your diseases,
who redeems your life from the Pit,
     who crowns you with steadfast love and
     mercy,
who satisfies you with good as long as you live.
     Amen. (Ps. 103:1-5a)

Blessing

ACT OF PREPARATION AT A PREVIOUS SERVICE
(a)
L: When you are offering your gift at the altar,
    if you remember that your brother or sister
      has something against you,
    leave your gift there before the altar and go;
    first be reconciled to your brother or sister,
    and then come and offer your gift. (Mt. 5:23-24)

Silent prayer

All: Have mercy on me, O God,
    according to your steadfast love.
    For I know my transgressions, and my sin is
        ever before me.
    Create in me a clean heart, O God,
        and put a right spirit within me.
            (Ps. 51:1a, 3, 10)

L: I declare in the name of Jesus that we are
    forgiven, loved, and free.

(b) *people may reply individually or corporately*
Brothers and sisters,
            if you will to love God before all things,
                in the power of God's Word,
            and to subject your will to God's will;
            then let each say: I will.

If you will love and serve your neighbors,
            and lay down your life in the power of
                our Lord Jesus Christ,
            who laid down his life for us,
            then let each say: I will.

If you will practice mutual admonition toward
        your brothers and sisters,
            speak and hear the truth,
            make peace with those whom you have
                offended,
            cease what causes harm to your neighbors,
            and do good to your enemies,
            then let each say: I will.

If you desire to confirm before the church this
　　pledge of love,
　　　　by eating bread and drinking wine,
　　　　the living memorial of the death of Jesus,
　　　　　our Lord,
　　　　then let each say: I desire it in the power
　　　　　of God.

Silent reflection

Let us eat and drink with one another in the
　　name of God the Father, the Son, and the
　　Holy Spirit.
May God give to all of us the strength to carry out
　　our pledge. Amen.[39]

OTHER WORDS OF INVITATION
(a)
Friends, this is the joyful feast of the people of
　　God!
They will come from east and west, and from
　　north and south,
　　　　and sit at table in the kingdom of God.
When our risen Lord was at table with his disciples,
　　he took the bread, and blessed and broke it,
　　and gave it to them.
Then their eyes were opened and they recognized
　　him.
This is the Lord's table.

Our Savior bids those who trust him and have
gone through the waters of baptism
to share the feast he has prepared.[40]

(b)
Jesus declared,
"For the bread of God is that which comes
down from heaven
and gives life to the world."
The people responded,
"Sir, give us this bread always."
Jesus answered,
"I am the bread of life.
Whoever comes to me will never be hungry,
and whoever believes in me will never be
thirsty." (Jn. 6:33-35)

OTHER COMMUNION PRAYERS

(a)
Almighty God, Creator of heaven and earth,
you formed us in your image;
you made a covenant with us to be our God.
When we had turned aside from your way and
abused your gifts,
you gave us, Jesus, your crowning gift.
Emptying himself, that our joy might be full,
he fed the hungry, healed the afflicted,
ate with the scorned and forgotten,
washed the disciples' feet,
and gave a holy meal as the pledge of his
abiding presence.

By the baptism of his suffering, death, and resurrection
> you gave birth to your church,
> delivered us from slavery to sin and death,
> and made with us a new covenant, by
> water and the Spirit.

And so, in remembrance of these your mighty
acts in Jesus Christ,
> we offer ourselves to you in praise as a
> living sacrifice.

Pour out your Holy Spirit on us, gathered here.

Grant us the communion of the body and blood
of Christ,
> that we may be for the world the body of
> Christ, redeemed by his blood.

By your Spirit make us one with Christ, one with
each other, and one in ministry to all the world,
> until Christ comes in final victory and we
> feast at his heavenly banquet.
> In his name we pray, Our Father ...[41]

(b)

Holy God, Lord of creation,
> you formed the earth from chaos;
>> you molded us in your image.

With mercy higher than the mountains and grace
deeper than the seas
> you called and led your people.

When we chose to flee your calling,
> you came to us through the life and death
> of the Messiah, Jesus, and adopted us
> as your own.

With bread and wine Jesus sealed your covenant
  with us.
Gathered at his table, we remember his life lived
  and offered up for others.
          In dying, he set us free from death.
          In rising, he opened the way to eternal life.
Send now your Holy Spirit on us and on this meal,
          that we might feed on Christ and share
              his bounty with the world.
We ask this through our Savior,
          who taught us to pray, saying, Our Father ...[42]

(c) *With sung responses (one or more verses of each
hymn; the prayer includes the words of institution and
has no separate prayers of thanks)*
Suggested hymn: "Let all mortal flesh keep
silence," HWB 463

Everlasting God, it is right that we should give
  you thanks and glory:
    you are the one God, living and true.
Through all eternity you live in unapproachable
  light.
Source of life and goodness,
    you have created all things to fill your crea-
        tures with every blessing
    and lead all people to the joyful vision of your
        light.

Countless hosts of angels stand before you to do
   your will;
they look upon your splendor and praise you,
night and day.
United with them, and in the name of every crea-
   ture under heaven,
      we too praise your glory as we sing:

Suggested hymn: "Holy, Holy, Holy!" HWB 120

Redeeming God, you so loved the world that in
   the fullness of time
      you sent the Beloved to be our Savior.
He was conceived by the power of the Holy
   Spirit,
      and born of the Virgin Mary, a human
         being like us in all things but sin.
To the poor he proclaimed the good news of
   salvation,
      to prisoners, freedom,
      and to those in sorrow, joy.
In fulfillment of your will he gave himself up to
   death;
      he freely offered himself as a scapegoat
         for the sins of the world.
By rising from the dead, he destroyed death and
   restored life.

Suggested hymn: "For God so loved us," HWB 167

That we might live no longer for ourselves but for
Christ,

> he sent the Holy Spirit from you, loving
> God, as his first gift to those who
> believe,
>
> to complete his work on earth and bring
> us the fullness of grace.

May the Holy Spirit sanctify us so that in the
breaking of the bread and the drinking of
the cup

> we might share the body and blood of
> Christ,
>
> the great mystery which Jesus left us as
> an everlasting covenant.

(pause)

While they were at supper, Jesus took bread, said
the blessing,

> broke the bread, and gave it to his disciples,
> saying, "Take this, all of you, and eat it:
> this is my body which will be given up
> for you."

In the same way, he took the cup, filled with wine.
He gave you thanks, and giving the cup to his
disciples,

> said, "Take this, all of you, and drink from it:
> this is the cup of my blood, the blood of
> the new and everlasting covenant.

It will be shed for you and for all so that
    sins may be forgiven.
    Do this in memory of me."
Let us proclaim the mystery of faith:

Suggested hymn: "This is the threefold truth,"
HWB 335

Lord, gather all who share this one bread
    and one cup into the one body of Christ, a
    living sacrifice of praise.

Communion

Suggested hymns: "Become to us the living
bread" (HWB 475), "Jesus, sun and shield art
thou," (HWB 466), and others.[43]

(d)
O Holy Trinity, your dance of love encircles and
    embodies us,
        drawing us into the mysteries of death and
        life, pain and hope, despair and joy.
When you offered yourself up for us, O Christ,
    you gave life the victory over death,
        hope the victory over pain,
        joy the victory over despair.
We thank you for creating the fruits of the earth,
    O God,

and for using these gifts of bread and
wine that we might know your
unending love.
Show yourself through our sharing of these gifts.
Good Spirit, come upon us now that we might
take Christ's body and blood into our bodies.
Dance in us, O Holy Trinity, as we eat and drink
this meal of grace,
that our bodies may be joined in one Body,
and that our earthly dance may be united
with yours. Amen.[44]

OTHER PRAYERS OF THANKS
(may be said separately or together)

(a)
For the bread:
Holy and Loving God,
we thank you for giving us this loaf,
your sign of Jesus' body broken for our
sins and raised for our salvation.
May all who eat this loaf be fed with the bread of
heaven. Amen.

For the cup:
Gracious God,
we thank you for giving us this cup,
your sign of Jesus' blood, poured out for
our healing.
May all who taste this wine drink from the cup of
salvation. Amen.

(b)

For the bread:

God of the fertile fields, God of the bread of life,
   your mercy and goodness overflow each day,
      filling us with a harvest of love.
Seas of wheat, streams of rain, waves of heat
      yield the staff of life, bread of body and soul.
This bread of Christ is blessed by earth, hand,
   and heaven.
May your Spirit feed us with this bread,
   nourishing body, mind, heart, and spirit.
May she form us in the image of Christ for the
   sake of the world. Amen.

For the cup:

God of ripe vineyards, God of our true vine,
      your faithfulness roots our lives, holding
         us with patience and grace.
Trimmed vines, enduring sun, watchful eyes
      yield the fruit of the vine, drink of body
      and soul.
The cup of Christ is blessed by earth, hand, and
   heaven.
May your Spirit satisfy us with this cup,
      quenching the thirsts of body, mind, heart,
      and spirit.
May she pour into us the image of Christ that we
   may be poured out for the world. Amen.[45]

Other Words Before the Distribution

The bread which we break, is it not a communion with the body of Christ?

The cup which we share, is it not a communion with the blood of Christ? (1 Cor. 10:16)

OTHER POST-COMMUNION PRAYERS

(a)

Bountiful God, you have nourished us with our Savior Christ who has come to us in this holy banquet.

Unite us now in faith, mercy, and justice.

Inspire us to love the world as Christ does.

Encourage us with the hope of everlasting life.

All this we ask, holy God, through Jesus Christ your incarnate word,

and your life-giving Spirit, one God forever and ever. Amen.[46]

(b) (to be used on Good Friday)

Christ our victim,

whose beauty was disfigured
and whose body torn upon the cross;
open wide your arms
to embrace our tortured world,
that we may not turn away our eyes,
but abandon ourselves to your mercy,
Amen.[47]

(c)

Eternal God,

> you have graciously accepted us as living members of your Son our Savior Jesus Christ,

> and you have fed us with spiritual food in the sacrament of his body and blood.

Send us now into the world in peace,

> and grant us strength and courage to love and serve you with gladness
> and singleness of heart;
> through Christ our Lord. Amen.[48]

(d)

God of abundance, you have fed us with the bread of life and the cup of salvation;

> you have united us with Christ and one another

> and made us one with all your people in heaven and on earth.

Now send us forth in the power of your Spirit,

> that we may proclaim your redeeming love to the world

> and walk in the resurrection of Christ our Savior. Amen.[49]

Other Prayers of Confession

(a) *(appropriate for Lent)*

L: Life is made up of aspiration and struggle,
        joy and lament,
        achieving and falling short.
    [During Lent,] we concern ourselves especially
        with those parts of ourselves
            and the world
                in which we struggle, lament, and
                fall short.
    We do this before the cross of Christ:
        he gave up his life to make others whole.
    We gather here because God has promised to
        change us more and more
            into people who live for him and for
            the world.
    Let us name what keeps us from living the
    new life God has promised.

Pause after each statement below

P: We have not loved God fully nor our
        neighbor as ourselves.
    We have grieved the Holy Spirit by settling
        for less than she offers or asks.
    We have taken refuge in worldly goods and
        comforts.
    We have let other people take the risks.
    We have been ashamed to name the name of
        Christ.

L: I therefore invite us to confess our sins to God.

P: Have mercy on me, O God, according to your steadfast love,

> for I know my transgressions and my sin is ever before me.

Create in me a clean heart, O God, and put a right spirit within me.

Silence

L: In the name of Jesus, I assure you that you are forgiven, loved, and free. Amen.

P: In the name of Jesus, we assure you that you are forgiven, loved, and free. Amen.

(b) *(silence may follow each petition, up to "heal our infirmities")*

All: Faithful God, whose mercy never ends,

> we confess that our will to serve you is imperfect.

We choose actions that honor ourselves.

We succumb to the temptations of power and greed.

We believe that our own work will save us.

We belittle the goodness of creation.

We mar the witness of the church with our pettiness.

We do not trust the Spirit's work in our midst.

Heal our infirmities, we pray.

Give us the mind of Christ.

By your Spirit work in us what pleases you. For Jesus' sake. Amen.

L: Brothers and sisters, God has forgiven us; we are set free. Let joy abound. Amen.[50]

Prayer of Humble Access

Father, we come boldly to the table of your Son,
> not trusting in ourselves that we are righteous,
>
> but trusting only in you and in your great mercy.

We are not fit even to eat the crumbs that fall from your table.

But you, O Lord, never change.

Your mercy never fails.

Feed us with the spiritual food of Christ's body and blood,
> that we may always abide in him and he in us. Amen.

Blessing

"**B**lessed be the God and Father of our Lord Jesus Christ, who has blessed us in Christ with every spiritual blessing in the heavenly places" (Eph. 1:3). A significant opportunity for ministry for the church and those who minister on its behalf are those occasions when the blessing of God is invoked. Though there are many opportunities to convey blessing, they are particularly available when covenants are made and life passages and milestones are marked. The benediction of God is called for at weddings; anniversaries; the consecration of children and their parents; the transition of children to adolescence and adulthood; the beginning of new educational, service, or business ventures; retirements; farewells; and other occasions.

Conveying God's blessing is a rich practice that is deeply embedded in the Bible and Christian custom. Out of the abundance of God's goodness, we seek God's blessing and invoke the lavish provision and well-being of God on persons, ventures, events, and activities. In the Old Testament, the root for blessing is fruitfulness (e.g., Gen. 1:22, 28). The Bible urges us to seek and expect God's blessing of fruitfulness in a wide variety of situations and activities.

Seeking God's benediction embraces and draws on the goodness of God that undergirds and sustains all of life. The foundational blessing of God is unsolicited and unconditional since "the world has been created good because God is good and provides all that is needed for life."[51] It flows out of the continuous, dynamic processes of life that were set in motion at creation, and the promise that God is with us in every circumstance (Ps. 139, Mt. 28). The possibility of life itself is a reflection of God's blessing on all of creation. "God blessed them, and God said to them, 'Be fruitful'" (Gen. 1:28).

From this inexhaustible wellspring of goodness, we seek to evoke and invoke God's well-being and provision in everything that we do. There are also ceremonial settings, where particular words and actions are used that, in the experience of God's people, convey and help to release the blessing of God. For example, Numbers 6:24 invokes God's blessing with these words: "The Lord bless you and keep you; the Lord make his face to shine upon you, and be gracious to you; the Lord lift up his countenance upon you, and give you peace."

The following words and actions are commended to us as powerful and empowering expressions of God's goodness and are means of releasing that goodness into our human experience. It is the witness of God's people over many centuries that carefully chosen words, ritual actions, and the human agents that speak and act on the behalf of God combine to release God's blessing into a wide variety of human experiences. Seeking God's blessing serves to stimulate our imaginations and enlarge our expectations of the One "who by the power at work within us is able to accomplish abundantly far more than all we can ask or imagine" (Eph. 3:20).

But these words and actions are not magical; they are not inherently effective and self-fulfilling. We seek God's blessing in faith without taking the blessing we seek for granted or diminishing the appropriate place of our responsibility for our own well-being. Nevertheless, it is the witness of the Bible, and of God's people throughout the ages, that particular words and acts of blessing, and the persons who invoke them, serve to release God's blessing in our lives.

The ministry of blessing in the church is informed and enriched by the example and ministry of Jesus. We recall the blessing of Jesus on the water that was turned into wine at the wedding at Cana, the blessing of the bread and the fish in the feeding of the multitudes, the blessing of children, and the blessing of the bread and the cup at the Last Supper. We also recognize the call of Jesus to bless those who curse us (Lk. 6:28) and the blessing pronounced upon the poor, the mourners, and those who are persecuted for the sake of Jesus (Mt. 5:11). For Jesus, blessing is more than success and well-being as defined by the world; it involves more than the comforts of material gain or the absence of pain. For Christians, every blessing that is sought and received is grounded in the reality of the cross and the victory of the resurrection of Christ, and it anticipates the eschatological fulfillment of God's promises.

The following are specific occasions when God's blessing might be invoked:

Marriage and Celibacy. "We believe that God intends human life to begin in families and to be blessed through families." "Families of faith are called to be a blessing to all the families of the earth." The worship context of a wedding, the songs, the prayers, and the ceremony provide multiple opportunities to seek the blessings of God on the marriage partners, their families, and the gathered congregation. The blessing on a marriage includes joy in companionship, faithfulness in keeping the marriage vows, courage in the face of adversity, fruitfulness in service, and fertility if the couple is called to have children. We should also be reminded that these blessings of marriage should not be so construed that those who are unmarried are excluded from God's blessing, for "we hold that within the church family, the goodness of being either single or married is honored."[52]

The blessing of children in their coming into the care of the church family and in their

development. It is a time-honored tradition that young children are brought before God's people for God's blessing (Lk. 2:22; 18:15a). This is also an appropriate time for parents to renew their commitment to be godly parents. Some congregations have also found it valuable to renew this consecration at important milestones in the children's lives, such as beginning school, celebrating the twelfth birthday, or high school graduation. In some congregations where people come forward to receive communion, children are encouraged to come forward with their parents to receive a blessing.

New educational, employment, or business ventures. As people begin these new ventures, we may choose to seek God's blessing upon them, that their efforts might be fruitful for the work and reign of God and that they might be good stewards of time, natural resources, and whatever financial gain may come their way.

Retirement. As people move to closure of significant work and career undertakings, we would do well to seek God's blessing upon them for what they have achieved. We would also seek for them grace and wisdom in the adjustments facing them, continued and new opportunities to experience the goodness of life, and opportunities for service.

Anniversaries. Wedding anniversaries, work and service anniversaries, anniversaries that mark important accomplishments (e.g., sobriety of an alcoholic) are important occasions on which to recall God's blessing in our lives. They rightly evoke expressions of gratitude and affirmation, and they remind everyone of the blessing that comes with faithfully keeping covenant commitments.

Farewells and sendings. In an age of increased mobility, it is good that we find more ways to deliberately seek God's blessing on people as they move to new locations. These often involve significant elements of loss and grief, but we should recognize both that God is going with them and that God will not leave us alone.

WEDDINGS

A Christian wedding is a public service of worship recognizing the commitment of two people who covenant to love each other faithfully and to live together within God's love to their mutual benefit. It is God who joins the couple, but those who attend the wedding agree, by their presence, to offer them encouragement and support.

The content and character of the marriage service should be appropriate for a service of worship and be primarily determined by the officiating minister. There are, however, good reasons for the prospective bride and groom to have a significant role in the creation of the service. Such investment can be a fruitful learning experience that will increase their understanding of the deeper meanings of marriage. Ownership in the ideas expressed and the language chosen by the couple can increase their degree of participation in the service and their own sense that the service is especially for them.

A wedding has such profound and immediate meaning to the couple and to their loved ones that great pastoral concern is required in making the service truly expressive of the couple while setting it within a greater theological and liturgical frame of reference. Historically, the role of ritual is to join us to others and to give us common words and gestures. Modern western people try to create unique rituals that isolate people from the tradition of common rituals and accentuate their individuality. Each couple is an expression of a universal pattern. If the couple write their own vows, they should still express values common to all Christian weddings.

The service need not be elaborate or expensive to be meaningful and beautiful. The tendency of our culture is to make a wedding into a flamboyant display. The pressure to do so is so strong that the minister does well to give couples and their families permission and encouragement to plan a simple wedding.

A wedding is first of all a worship service. People gather to thank God for the love given to a man and a woman, to ask God's blessing on their vows, and to pledge support for the couple's intentions. Planning for the occasion should be based on this three-fold purpose.

Couples will sometimes ask to receive communion. The Lord's Supper is inherently communal, so if it is celebrated, the whole congregation should be included. This is complicated in a pluralistic society by the fact that non-Christians will likely be present. If there is to be communion, care should be taken to inform guests as to the meaning of the Lord's Supper.

Wedding customs among Mennonites have varied greatly. It may be said, however, that traditionally, wedding services followed the regular order of worship—with congregational singing, Scripture reading, and preaching. The couple, usually without attendants, entered together as the service began, often to the singing of a hymn. This pattern is recommended because it makes clear that the wedding is a service whose focus is the worship of God and the calling down of blessing on the couple. Through the singing of hymns and other such actions, the congregation becomes an indispensible participant in what happens. In some Mennonite areas, weddings were part of a regular Sunday service. The "giving away of the bride" is an Anglo-Saxon institution without roots in Mennonite tradition. In the contemporary reform of marriage rites, most denominations recommend that the couple enter together. New ways of parents and families blessing the couple have developed.

As one who presides at weddings of both members and nonmembers, the minister should develop a pastoral relationship with the couple before and after the wedding. Premarital counseling, which includes preparation for marriage and planning for the service as well as early follow-up after the wedding, should be scheduled by the minister.

If a minister is asked to officiate at a wedding in a church where he or she is not currently serving as pastor, professional courtesy requires that the invitation not be considered unless it comes with the consent of the pastor in whose church the wedding will take place. The officiating minister should suggest to the couple that their own pastor be included.

Whether in the minister's own church or elsewhere, congregational policies regarding weddings, receptions, the use of the building, and fees should be made clear to the couple and minister(s) at the time negotiations to perform the marriage service are held.

Marriage laws differ. Before consenting to preside at a wedding in any jurisdiction, the minister should become informed about marriage laws so as to comply fully with them. The presider is responsible to see to it that documents are promptly signed and returned.

The minister and the couple should be clear

with each other about the real starting time of the service. The use of music, candles, flowers, and other symbols in the service should be carefully reviewed so that selections appropriate to marriage and the worship of God are chosen. The complexity of family systems that may include the presence of divorced or remarried parents, as well as children from previous unions, makes it important that the role of family members in the service be clarified. The bride and groom need to negotiate these understandings with the minister and with their families before the rehearsal.

Printed orders of service are helpful when they include congregational participation and the names of those in the wedding party. The taking of flash pictures or the presence of photographers moving around during the service is disruptive.

The minister is in charge of the wedding rehearsal. Suggestions for changes in the service during the rehearsal should come only from the bride and groom. It is helpful to begin the rehearsal with prayer.

The full service need not be rehearsed word for word, but going through entrances, location of participants, movements, cues, and a sampling of words will allow for a feeling of confidence in what will happen during the service. All concerned will then have greater freedom to participate in the actual wedding.

Hymns:

"Come, let us all unite to sing" (HWB 12)

"Where charity and love prevail" (HWB 305)

"Will you let me be your servant" (HWB 307)

"Jesu, joy of man's desiring" (HWB 604)

"When love is found" (HWB 623)

"O perfect love" (HWB 624)

"Your love, O God, has called us" (HWB 625)

"Hear us now, O God, our maker" (HWB 626)

Scripture passages:

Genesis 1:26-31a	Mark 10:6-9
Psalm 67	John 15:9-17
Psalm 112:1-6	Romans 12:1-2, 9-13 (14-20)
Psalm 148	1 Corinthians 13
Song of Solomon 2:10-13	Ephesians 5:21-32
Tobit 8:4-8	Colossians 3:12-17
Matthew 5:1-10	1 John 4:7-12 (13-19)
Matthew 22:35-40	

Visual setting:

. If the congregation has a festive wedding banner in neutral colors, this can be displayed. It is customary for the couple to choose flowers, plants, candles, and other visual symbols. The pastor may encourage simplicity. If any of the parents of the couple are deceased, consider a simple remembrance, such as a lit candle, flower, or plant.

THE WEDDING SERVICE

Prelude

Processional music (if this is not a hymn, a hymn may follow)

Gathering the community

Grace be unto us and peace from God our Father
and the Lord Jesus Christ. Amen.

We have come together in the presence of God
to witness the wedding of _____
and _____
and to ask God to bless them.

This wedding is a celebration of marriage as a gift
of God in which two people become one
flesh.

It is a celebration of their promise to be loyal to
each other
without reservation, without end.

It is a celebration of a new time of life
and its responsibility for passing on beliefs
and values they hold
to the generation which will follow them.

_____ and _____ want to place this day and
their lives under the rule of Christ.

Let us pray that, by God's help, they might do so.

Opening prayer

Gracious God,
you have taught us through Jesus Christ
that love is the fulfilling of the law.

Grant to these your servants

---

that loving one another
they may continue in your love
until their lives' end;
through Jesus Christ our Lord. Amen.

Music
Scripture
Sermon
Music
Declaration of intent (the wedding party stands)
L: _____, will you give yourself to _____, to
be her husband:

> to love her, comfort her, honor and protect
> her;
> and forsaking all others, be faithful to her
> so long as you both shall live?

Groom: I will.

L: _____, will you give yourself to
_____, to be his wife:

> to love him, comfort him, honor and pro-
> tect him;
> and forsaking all others, to be faithful to
> him so long as you both shall live?

Bride: I will.

L: Do you, parents/children [of previous
unions] of the families of _____
and _____, give your blessing
to this marriage?
Families: We do.

L: Will you as a congregation do all in your power to support and uphold this marriage?

P: We will.

Vows

Groom: I, _____, take you, _____, to be my wife.
I promise before God and these friends
to be your loving and faithful husband,
to share with you in plenty and in want,
in joy and in sorrow,
in sickness and in health,
and to join with you so that together we
may serve God and others,
as long as we both shall live.

Bride: I, _____, take you, _____, to be my husband.
I promise before God and these friends
to be your loving and faithful wife,
to share with you in plenty and in want,
in joy and in sorrow,
in sickness and in health,
and to join with you so that together we
may serve God and others,
as long as we both shall live.

SAND

Rings may be silently exchanged or given with the following words:

Groom: _____, I give you this ring as a symbol of my vow.

With all that I am and all that I have, I honor you.

Bride: _____, I give you this ring as a symbol of my vow.

With all that I am and all that I have, I honor you.

Pronouncement

I declare that you are husband and wife, in the name of the Father, Son, and Holy Spirit. Amen.

What God has joined together let no one put asunder.

[kiss]

Blessing of the couple (the couple may kneel and the minister may place hands on their heads)

May God bless you and keep you;

May the very face of God shine upon you,
and be gracious to you.

May God's presence embrace you
and give you peace. Amen.

Prayer

Most gracious God,

we give you thanks for your tender love in sending Jesus Christ to come among us,

to be born of a human mother,

and to make the way of the cross to be
the way of life.
We thank you also for consecrating the union of
man and woman in his name.
By the power of your Holy Spirit,
pour out the abundance of your blessing
on _____ and _____.
Defend them from every enemy. Lead
them into all peace.
Let their love for each other be a seal
upon their hearts,
a mantle about their shoulders, and a
crown upon their foreheads.
Bless them in their work
and in their companionship;
in their sleeping and in their
waking;
in their joys and in their sorrows;
in their life and in their death.
Finally, in your mercy, bring them to that
table where your saints feast forever
in your heavenly home;
through Jesus Christ our Lord, who
taught us to pray, saying, Our Father ...[53]

Blessing of the congregation
The grace of our Lord Jesus Christ,
the love of God,
and the communion of the Holy Spirit be
with us all. Amen.

Hymn (as a recessional or before an instrumental recessional)
Postlude

Other Wedding Resources

Blessing by parents
L: Who now present this man and woman to be married and bless their union?
Parents: We do.

Vows
Groom: I, _____, take you, _____, to be my wife,
to have and to hold from this day forward;
for better, for worse,
for richer, for poorer,
in sickness and in health,
to love and to cherish
for the rest of our lives,
according to God's holy law.
This is my solemn vow.

Bride: I, _____, take you, _____, to be my husband,
to have and to hold from this day forward;
for better, for worse,
for richer, for poorer,
in sickness and in health,
to love and to cherish
for the rest of our lives,
according to God's holy law.
This is my solemn vow.

Blessing of the couple

Blessed are you, mothering God,
in your great love you created us male and female
and made the union of husband and wife
an image of the union between you and your
    people.
You sent Jesus Christ to come among us,
making your love visible in him,
to bring new life to the world.

Send your Holy Spirit to pour out
the abundance of your blessing on _____ and

_____,
who have this day given themselves
to each other in marriage.

Bless them in their work
and in their companionship;
    in their sleeping and in their waking;
    in their joys and in their sorrows;
    in their life and in their death.

Give them the gift and heritage of children
in accordance with your will,
and make their home a haven of peace.

Bless them
so that all may see in their lives together
in the community of your people
a vision of your kingdom on earth.
And finally, in the fullness of time,
welcome them into the glory of your presence.
Through your Son Jesus Christ. Amen.[54]

THE CONSECRATION OF
PARENTS AND INFANTS

The birth of children has to do with God's work in both creation and redemption. In the act of consecration, we praise God "for it was you who formed my inward parts; you knit me together in my mother's womb. I praise you, for I am fearfully and wonderfully made" (Ps. 139:13-14a). In this act, we also bring the newborn child into a relationship with the body of Christ. The nature of this relationship has been a source of disagreement between churches which baptize infants and those which do not. For the latter, the act of consecration is a declaration that the atoning work of Christ includes all who are born. They remain in a state of grace until the age of accountability when they come to their own faith in Christ or choose another way. When infants are presented to God and to the church, they are placed in the care of the church. With Christian parents, the children can grow up with and into their parents' faith. In the service of consecration, the parents commit themselves to this calling.

Jesus made children a model of faith (Mk. 10:13-16). Their dependant and trusting natures make them receptive to God's presence in their lives. It is the task of families and the church to nurture this faith and to prepare children for a more mature time in life when they heed the call of Christ and accept Christ's claim on their lives.

The consecration of parents and infants belongs in the regular Sunday assembly, on one of the first Sundays on which the infants are brought to church. Parents, as well as the congregation, should be prepared beforehand for the promises they are about to make. Because both the parents and the congregation are asked to commit themselves to the material and spiritual well-being of the child, this service can be meaningful only to parents who have a living faith in Christ and actively participate in the church. This is sometimes true of only one parent; if the other parent does not stand in the way of the spouse's commitment, the service of consecration still carries its intended meaning (1 Cor. 7:12-14). This is also true, of course, in situations where the child lives with only one of its parents. Churches that baptize believers only have shied away from sponsors because of their association with infant baptism. In most cases, the congregation is appropriately seen as the sponsor. There is, however, no theological reason for ruling out sponsors if, like the parents, they have a living faith in Christ and are active participants in the church. If this is not the case, the act of consecration becomes a social ritual in which the essential spiritual intention is displaced. This service is the entrance way to the Christian pilgrimage.

Hymns:

"For the beauty of the earth" (HWB 89)

"Lord of our growing years" (HWB 479)

"Shepherd of tender youth" (HWB 480)

"Child of blessing, child of promise" (HWB 620)

"Jesus, friend so kind and gentle" (HWB 621)

"Wonder of wonders" (HWB 622)

Scripture passages:

Mark 10:13-16   Luke 2:21-40

Visual setting:

Consider creating a banner (quilted, painted, appliqued, etc.) that will be displayed whenever the congregation consecrates an infant. One of the strongest visual symbols of consecration is the minister holding the child. The minister may walk with the child through the congregation, introducing the child to the church family while the congregation sings a hymn of welcome. Siblings of the new infant may be invited to come to the front with the parents and infant. A single flower, such as a rosebud, may announce the birth or consecration of a baby.

The Service (parent/s and minister stand together before the congregation)

M: When Christian parents present their child to God before the congregation,

they come to thank God for the life entrusted to them,

to offer their child back to God and to ask for God's blessing on their life together.

We as a congregation come to share their joy,
>to pray with them for the child's well-being and to receive him/her into the care of the church.

Like Hannah and Mary of old, you have
>brought your child here to consecrate it to God.

You have come to offer _____ into the
>strong and tender providence of God
>>and the nurture of the church.

Prayer
Gracious God:
like a father who nurtures his children
you have cared for us;
like a mother you have called us by name
and claimed us as your own;
you have loved us into being,
placed us in human families,
and blessed us on our journey.
By the presence of your Spirit
consecrate this child/these children and parent/s
for their journey together through life,
through Jesus Christ our Savior. Amen.[55]

The Questions (to the parents)
L: Do you accept your child as a gift from of God?
Parents: I/We do.

L: Do you dedicate yourself/yourselves as a/

parent/s to bring up your child in the nurture
and admonition of the Lord, preparing him/her
to come to an open confession of Christ?

Parents: I/We do.

L: Do you promise to gladly surrender your
child to the ministry God has in mind for
him/her, even if it might involve going to the
ends of the earth?

Parents: I/We do.

[Optional question to sponsor/s:

L: Will you see that this child is nurtured in the
faith of the church, and by your prayers and
witness guide it into the full stature of Christ?

Sponsors: I/We will.]

L: (to the congregation): Do you accept responsibility for the well-being of this child, will you
by prayer, example, and words support
her/his parent/s in nurturing this child to
respond to the grace and truth that are in
Christ?

P: We will.

The Act of Consecration

L: (<u>name/s, of parent/s</u>), may the God who has
entrusted you with this child grant you fullness of love in raising it.

   May God grant you to live a life of faithfulness to the gospel before your children so that
they might know the way of the kingdom.

(The minister takes the child into his or her arms and prays:)

_____, the God who created you, who sent his Son to redeem you, and his Spirit to dwell in you,

> may this God watch over you, enabling you to seek, to find, and to know him.

(The minister places a hand on the child's head and prays:)

_____, may God bless you and keep you;

May the very face of God shine upon you,

> and be gracious to you.

May God's presence embrace you

> and give you peace. Amen.

Other Resources for the Consecration of Parents and Children

Alternate words of consecration

(a)

Tender God, accept _____, who has been brought to you for consecration.

> Grant that as she/he grows in years,
>> she/he may also grow in the grace and knowledge of the Lord Jesus Christ.

> By the influence of your Holy Spirit, may she/he become a child of God,
>> serving you faithfully all the days of his/her life.

> We ask this through the same Christ who

lives and reigns with you and the Holy
Spirit, one God forever and ever. Amen.
(followed by Aaronic blessing)

(b)

_____, may the love of God, the gracious
Spirit of Christ,
and the fellowship of God's people bless your
life.

Prayer for an adopted child
God, you have adopted all of us as your children.
We give you thanks for _____, who has come
to bless this family and for the parent/s who
(has/have) welcomed this child as
(her/his/their) own. By the power of your Holy
Spirit, fill their home with love, trust, and understanding, through Jesus Christ. Amen.[56]

Prayer said by the parents
Our heavenly Father, we thank you for our child. We
accept _____ as a sacred trust. Give us divine
resources to nurture, to love, to counsel, to teach, to
train, to show. Give us your Spirit with strength and
wisdom. May our child one day receive Jesus as
Savior and Lord. We surrender _____ to you, to
be kept by your power, to be used in your service,
and finally, to be received into your presence.
Through Jesus Christ, our Lord. Amen.[57]

Additional resources may be found in HWB 791-792.

OTHER SERVICES OF BLESSING

Each of the following may take place in public worship, in a small group, or in private. There is a long Mennonite tradition in favor of silver, golden, and diamond anniversaries as services in their own right. Where any of these acts of blessing happens as part of a regular service, it is appropriate for participants to gather together at the front of the meeting place to focus attention on those who have come to seek God's blessing. Gestures may accompany each of these events:

- Anointing (see the **Anointing** section)
- Exchange of peace (the holy kiss, embrace, hand of fellowship)
- Sign of the cross. Protestants have generally rejected this ancient and primal Christian gesture because of its association with exaggerated ceremonialism in the late medieval church. This understandable reaction should not determine present-day Mennonite practice of such a profoundly simple evocation of Christ. The minister may either trace a cross on the person's forehead, or may make the sign of the cross over the person's body (without touching), beginning at the forehead, going down to the solar plexus, and then from one shoulder to the other, usually accompanying the words "In the name of the Father, and of the Son, and of the Holy Spirit. Amen." The act is a modest one, a wordless mediation of the triune God's

presence.
- One or both hands extended onto head or shoulders

The statements and prayers may be spoken by one or by all present.

Blessing of a Life of Celibacy

While the church has always accepted celibacy along with marriage as equal ways of serving the Lord, Protestantism has seldom offered pastoral resources to people discerning if they are so called or public affirmation to those who believe they can best serve God in this way for a limited time or a lifetime. This service has a variety of potential uses, among them after a marriage has ended but the person is not ready to pursue another relationship, as part of a calling to ministry which may include commissioning or ordination. It may be a public or private occasion.

L: For just as the body is one and has many members,
and all the members of the body, though many, are one body,
so it is with Christ.[59]
For in the one Spirit, we were all baptized into one body—Jews or Greeks, slaves or free—
and were all made to drink of one Spirit.
Now there are varieties of gifts, but the same Spirit,

and there are varieties of services, but the
same Lord,
and there are varieties of activities but there is
the same God. (1 Cor. 12)

Jesus said concerning celibacy,
"Not everyone can accept this teaching, but only
those to whom it is given.
For there are eunuchs who have been so from
birth,
and there are eunuchs who have been made
eunuchs by others,
and there are eunuchs who have made themselves eunuchs for the sake of the kingdom of
heaven.
Let anyone accept this who can." (Mt. 19:11-12)
Our sister/brother, _____, believes that
she/he is called to a life/time of celibacy.
Are you so resolved to follow Christ in the spirit
of the Gospel
that your whole life may be a faithful witness to
God's love
and a convincing sign of the kingdom of heaven?
Answer: I am.

M: Do you receive celibacy as a gift and calling
from God?
Answer: I do.

Prayer
May God the Lord who called Abraham and

Sarah to set out not knowing where they were going shepherd you in your pilgrimage and lead you by safe pathways.

May God the Son, who in his earthly life was often solitary, be your constant companion.

May God the Spirit who helps us in our weakness teach you to pray as you ought and strengthen you in holiness of life. Amen.[58]

L: You are part of a chosen company within the flock of Christ.

Nourish your love of God by feeding on Christ and his Word.

Strengthen that love by self-denial, by the study of Scripture, and by prayer.

Let your thoughts be on the things of God.

You have died and your life is hidden with Christ in God.

Receive the new life which is given to you.

Be filled with love for the world.[59]

Acclamation (said first by the candidate, then by those who have made similar promises, then by the whole assembly)

Uphold me, O Lord, according to your promise and I shall live. Let not my hope be in vain.

(The person is presented with a Bible or a cross on behalf of those gathered.)

L: Receive this Bible/cross as a sign of devotion to Christ and his way. Go in peace.

Engagement to be Married

L: It is my pleasure to announce to you the engagement to be married of _____ and _____ [children of _____, of _____ church]. Let us pray for them as they prepare for marriage.

Reading of Scripture verse (Job 5:8-9; Song of Solomon 2:10-12; Psalm 37:5)

Engagement prayer (Sarah and Tobias, heroes of a romance in the book of Tobit [ch. 8], pray this prayer together at the close of their wedding day.)

L: Blessed are you, O God of our ancestors and blessed is your name in all generations forever.

Let the heavens and the whole creation bless you forever.

P: You made Adam and Eve as a help and support for each other.

From the two of them the human race has sprung.

You said, "It is not good that the man should be alone; let us make a partner for him like himself."

Couple: We now take each other, not because of lust but with sincerity.

Grant that we may find mercy and grow old together.

All: Amen.

Wedding Anniversaries

Appropriate Scriptures include Matthew 5:3-16; 1 Corinthinas 13; 1 John 4:7-19.

In your wedding vows, you promised each other love and faithfulness,

sharing in plenty and want, in joy and sorrow, in sickness and health,

joined together that you might serve God and others.

This is an occasion of thanksgiving for the mercies you have received,

the loyalties you have kept, the transgressions you have forgiven,

the hopes to which you have held fast.

We join together in thanking God for his steadfast love to you

and for your steadfast love to each other [and to your children].

Prayer

Blessed are you, O God, maker of the times and seasons of life.

We thank you for the gift of time
>and for all the days in which your favor has
>>rested on these your children.
Forgive their sins (*silence*),
>increase their love,
>>let their life together be a sign of the union
>>>between Christ and the church.
Grant that they may grow old together. For the
sake of your only Son, our Savior. Amen.

Widowhood
*Appropriate Scriptures include Psalm 71:6-9 and John
14:1-3.*

Prayer

Eternal God, eternal friend, your love is stronger
than death.

We mourn _____'s loss of _____, his/her
companion in life.

Yet we remember with gratitude their years
together.

In times of desolation send your comfort,
>in times of emptiness send your
>indwelling Spirit,
>in times of need send friends.

Uphold _____ in hope and in the promise of a
new heaven and a new earth,
>your dwelling place and ours.

For the sake of Jesus Christ who died and rose for
us. Amen.

Separation

Appropriate Scriptures include Psalm 31:1-5 and Matthew 10:29-31.

Prayer
(This prayer may be offered for both individuals together, for both separately, or for the one person asking for blessing.)

Merciful God, you made us for each other,
> for a life in which love is always to have the
> last word.

When our love falls short and cannot heal,
> we turn to your love for forgiveness and hope.

Speak to _____ in their/her/his sorrow.

Take away bitterness, grant peace, promise healing.

Let _____'s heart/s be set above all else on the
> coming of your kingdom.

[We bring you their children, _____, and place
> them in your hands.
>> Hold them close, protect them from all ill.]

For the sake of Jesus our Good Shepherd. Amen.

Retirement/Old Age

Appropriate Scriptures include Exodus 20:8-11; Psalm 71:6-9; Psalm 103:1-14, 17-18; Matthew 10:29-31; Sirach 44:1-15.

Prayer

Eternal God, you made our world good, and set
    the times for our labor and rest.
You made us for one another,
          and gave us talents to be used for the good
            of all [imaginativeness in creating,
          persistence in doing, wisdom in speaking,
          compassion in responding].
To all who come to Christ, you give gifts for the
    building up of the church and the good of the
    world
        [steadfastness in praying, power in
        healing, courage in obeying, joy in
        witnessing].
Grant our sister/brother _____ a sure sense of
    the good things you have brought about
        in and through her/him.
Grant him/her satisfaction from tasks
    accomplished.
Prepare him/her for new tasks in your kingdom.
Grant her/him eyes of faith to follow where love
    calls.
Through Jesus our Mighty Lord. Amen.

Final Illness

Appropriate Scriptures include Isaiah 43:16-21; Isaiah 46:3-4; 1 Corinthians 15:49; Psalm 31:14-16; Psalm 73:23-26.

Prayer

Receive a blessing for all that may be required of
you,

> that love may drive out fear,
> that you may be more perfectly aban-
> doned to the will of God,
> and that peace and contentment may
> reign in your heart,
> and through you may spread over the
> face of the earth.

The blessing of God,

> Giver of Life,
> Bearer of Pain,
> Maker of Love,
> Creator and Sustainer,
> Liberator and Redeemer,
> Healer and Sanctifier,

be with you and all whom you love both living
and departed,

> now and forever, through Christ our
> Lord. Amen.[60]

Farewell

L: When one of us suffers, we all suffer; when one of us is honored, we all rejoice. (1 Cor. 12:26)

Today _____ leave/s our city/neighborhood and congregation for another.

He/she/they have shared our faith, our struggles, our satisfactions.

In all his/her/their pursuits, _____ was/were being prepared for a new time of life.

We bless his/her/their decision to choose it.

Though we are sad to see you go, we understand your going as a sending.

You came to us, offered us your gifts, and received ours.

Take what you have found in our midst, and pass it on.

As you go, carry with you the good news of what God has done in Christ.

Find a community in which you can live the faith we have shared.

Remember us who serve here, support us with love and prayer as we will support you.

Prayer

Ancient of Days, you are our journey and our end.

Nowhere are we lost when we are with you.

Today we pray for your blessing on _____.

Inspire in him/her/them new responses to your call.

Protect him/her/them in uncertainty.

Grant him/her/them always the sure knowledge
    of being your child. In Jesus' name. Amen.

Blessing

The Lord will keep you from all evil; God will
    keep your life.

The Lord will keep your going out and your com-
    ing in

        from this time on and forevermore.
        Amen. (Ps. 121:7-8)

Blessing of a Meetinghouse

*The congregation assembles outside at the front door of
the meetinghouse. (In case of inclement weather, representatives of the congregation may carry out this act.)*

L: Lift up your heads, O gates! And be lifted up,
     O ancient doors!

P: That the king of glory may come in!

L: Who is the king of glory?

P: The Lord, strong and mighty, the Lord,
     mighty in battle!

All: Lift up your heads, O gates! And be lifted up,
     O ancient doors!

     That the king of glory may come in!

L: Almighty God, we thank you for making us
     in your image

        to share in the ordering of your world.

     Receive the work of our hands in this place

now to be set apart for your worship
    the building up of the living,
    and the remembrance of the dead,
    to the praise and glory of your name,
    through Jesus Christ our Lord. Amen.[61]

Congregation enters with an appropriate act of praise. In the service that follows, the litany of dedication may be used.

Litany of dedication

L: For the ministry of the word, for the worship of your name, for giving and receiving counsel, for participation in the ordinances of the church ...

P: We dedicate this house.

L: For warning against sin, for calling to salvation, for proclaiming the whole counsel of God ...

P: We dedicate this house.

L: For comfort to those who mourn, for help to those who are tempted, for strength to those who are weak, for celebration with those who are joyful ...

P: We dedicate this house.

L: For studying the Scriptures, for discerning God's will, for passing on the faith ...

P: We dedicate this house.

L: For voices of dissent when wrong is done, for voices of peace when violence threatens, for voices of song indwelled by the Spirit ...

P: We dedicate this house.
L: For your indwelling and empowering ...
P: We dedicate ourselves.
All: Thanks be to God through our Lord Jesus Christ. Amen.

Blessing for weddings, ordinations, and other appropriate occasions

May the presence of God's Spirit and of God's people,

in the (*occasion*) of _____ (and _____),
be above you to overshadow you
underneath you to uphold you
before you to guide you
behind you to encourage you
beside you to nurture you
within you to empower you
Amen.[62]

For diverse occasions

(a)
May the Holy Spirit dwell in your soul.
May Christ fill your heart and mind.
May God hold you in love, grace, and peace. Amen.[63]

(b)
God's blessing be with you,
Christ's peace be with you,
the Spirit's outpouring be with you, now and always. Amen.[64]

(c)
May God always bless us.
May Christ always shine through us.
May the Spirit always rest upon us. Amen.[65]

For a home
The blessing of a home can be an annual event, or done to inaugurate a new place of residence. The minister and other guests gather at the entrance and are welcomed by their hosts.

L: Let us begin in the name of the Father, the Son, and the Holy Spirit.
P: Amen.

The minister traces the sign of the cross on the door.
P: May this door always open in hospitality; may it always beckon to service.

A member of the household lights a candle.
P: May the light of Christ always shine in this home.

A member of the household presents a Bible.
P: May the word of God always be heard and heeded in this home.

L: May the Holy Spirit bless this home.
P: Both mortar and masonry.

L: Both stone and beam.
P: Both ridge and frame.
L: Both roof and foundation.
P: Both window and woodwork.

[L: Both young and old.
P: Both parents and children.]
This may be adjusted according to those who live in the home.

L: Both friend and stranger.
P: Both neighbor and guest.

Household: Bless us, O Lord, that we may find here shelter, peace, and health.
Make our house be a haven for all who enter it.
May all guests be received as Christ.

All: The Lord will keep your going out and your coming in from this time on and forevermore.

The Calling and Setting Apart of Leaders

The roots of ordination go back to the Hebrew Bible and the instructions given to Moses to consecrate Aaron and his sons as priests for the congregation of God's people (Ex. 29 and Lev. 8—10). Over a period of seven days, Israelites observed a prescribed series of washings, clothings, anointings, sacrifices, meals, and offerings until in the end, "Aaron lifted his hands toward the people and blessed them..., and the glory of the LORD appeared to all the people" (Lev. 9:22-23, NIV).

The New Testament does not give a clear prescriptive mandate for ordination as such, and some have, therefore, judged it as not essential or even as inappropriate for the Christian faith. However, there are numerous examples of Jesus and the church calling persons to ministry and service followed by a blessing and confirmation to such persons for their unique role and ministry. In the same way, the church "lays hands on" while offering prayers of commission and blessing (Acts 6:1-7; Acts 13:1-3; 2 Tim. 1:3-7).

The Holy Spirit is at work in the church and in the lives of individual Christians. A coincidence gradually emerges between an individual's inner calling to ministry and the church's call to that individual. Thus, an individual's readiness for ordination should not rest only on his or her personal conviction of being called, though this is indispensible. The readiness for ordination depends equally on the church's discernment that someone manifests the necessary gifts of the Spirit. The cumulative witness of both testaments is that in the setting apart of leaders, the church witnesses with the candidate to his/her calling and appeals to God to seal that calling with the presence and power of the Holy Spirit.

"Now there are varieties of gifts, but the same Spirit; and there are varieties of services, but the same Lord; and there are varieties of activities, but it is the same God who activates all of them in everyone" (1 Cor. 12:4-6). In conversion and baptism, everyone receives the Spirit and is called to ministry. Our purpose here is to offer resources for the calling and setting apart of one ministry, that of leadership. Across the centuries, the church has designated leadership roles differently. In the Mennonite church today, we honor lifelong vocational callings to ministry. We name this ordination. We also honor ministries that are not full time, not usually for a lifetime, and normally tied to a particular setting. We name this commissioning.

We are now at the end of a generation's debate, in our church and beyond it, concerning the meaning of ordination. The study process that led to *A Mennonite Polity for Ministerial Leadership*[66] issued a resounding affirmation of both ordained and commissioned ministries for the well-being of the church. Because ordination was subject to such scrutiny, it seems important to include here a summary of current Mennonite understanding of the subject.

It is significant to note that in both the Old Testament example and in the New Testament events what transpired benefited not only the individual(s) being consecrated. The setting apart was celebrated by the entire community of God's people and became the occasion for their own blessing and growth. Ministerial leadership is not, therefore, an end in itself but a means toward the welfare of the church.

The giving and receiving of credentials for ministry has to do with covenant making within the church. It is a three-way covenant involving God, the church, and those called by God and the church to serve in a ministerial leadership role.

Covenants are not private affairs, even though they are intensely personal. We enact covenants in ceremonies. We engage in symbolic actions to create a memory of the covenant for the continuing relationship.

Covenant making has to do with intentionality and promises within a sinful and fragile world. Those who engage in the forming of a new relationship within the covenant promise faithfulness, loyalty, love, and care for each other. In other words, they pledge mutual support along with a willingness to be accountable to each other.

Within the covenant of ordination, the person receiving the credentials for ministry promises to serve the church to the best of his/her ability according to the highest standards of Christian public service. It is a promise of faithfulness to the Christian gospel, of service to the church for its well-being and growth, and of loyalty to its Lord and Savior, Jesus Christ.

The church also makes promises within the covenant of ordination. It pledges openness of mind, body, and soul for Christian growth and service. It promises faithfulness as disciples of Jesus Christ, guided by the sacred Scriptures. It offers itself to be supportive in life-giving, ministry-enhancing ways to those who serve in a representational role.

When we speak of the church as the context and the partner in the covenant of ordination, we always mean the local congregation, the area conference, and the denomination. All are active participants in this covenant making of ministerial credentials.

A Mennonite Polity for Ministerial Leadership describes the meaning of ordination as follows: "When the church ordains a man or woman to ministerial leadership, it intends to say at least the following:

1. We confirm the call of God to the person being ordained for ministry within or on behalf of

the church. It is a time of blessing and celebration by the church for the gracious gifts of God to all, inasmuch as the ordained ministry is part of the ministry of the whole church.

2. We affirm the person for the unique leadership gifts the minister brings to the Christian community. We recognize the investment in spiritual, relational, and intellectual growth through completion of special training for this role within the church. We affirm a clarity of identity as shepherds of the church and servants of Jesus Christ.

3. We identify the person being ordained as one who represents God in a 'priestly' role within the community of faith where all are priests serving God (Rev. 1:6, 5:10). As such, we recognize the role of spiritual leadership within the church, a leadership growing out of an authentic humanity, and an authentic spirituality disciplined by a life of prayer, contemplation, and the Scriptures.

4. We entrust an office of ministry to the person being ordained. We thereby empower this person to act in a representative way on the church's behalf with both the privileges and the responsibilities of the office. With this ministerial office, we recognize an authority which is granted for leadership within the church. Paradoxically, this authority must constantly be earned by evidence of wisdom, competence, integrity, humility, and perception.

5. We call the person being ordained to particular tasks associated with this office: to preach

and teach; to lead with vision and wisdom; to equip members to release their spiritual gifts; to provide pastoral care, to be responsible for the church's rites of marriage, baptism, observance of the Lord's Table; and to help represent the church in the local community and in the conference.

6. Between the congregation and the person ordained we ask for a mutual accountability of support, respect, and care. For the person ordained, accountability to the church includes at least the following: personal moral integrity, faithfulness as stewards of the gospel, an exemplary life of equality and servanthood in relation to others, and effectiveness in exercising this ministry. The congregation covenants to pray for the ordained person, to give and receive counsel, to support his/her leadership ministry, and respect the authority of the office into which the minister has been ordained.

7. We declare our trust in the person being ordained by providing a credential for leadership ministry; the credential is primarily for service within the church, and secondly, is also acknowledged in society and by the state.

When the process of choosing and preparing a candidate has been completed, advance notice of the day of ordination should be given so that all those with a stake in the candidate's ministry may be present. It is sometimes advantageous to have the service on a Sunday afternoon so that people from outside the congregation may participate. Ordination is one of the great joys of the church and should be thus celebrated. The preferences of the candidate and the traditions of the ordaining congregation and conference should all be given their due in the planning of the service. The ordination service should be approached and planned with the expectation that God will be at work in this service to bless and empower the one to be ordained to faithful and fruitful service.

In Mennonite rituals and those of most denominations, there is a nearly uniform pattern of presentation, examination, prayer of consecration, and presentation of a Bible. Candidates for ordination to missionary work, chaplaincy, or ministry on behalf of an institution often minister in settings without a congregation. Square brackets in Form 1 designate aspects of the ceremony which might not be applicable to those callings.

ORDINATION FORM 1

Presentation

L: Brothers and sisters, we are gathered today in the presence of God and this assembly
to ordain _____ to the pastoral ministry.
Who presents _____ for ordination to ministry?

P: We present our sister/brother _____
to be set apart for [the] ministry [of this congregation] in the world.

Hymns:

"Tú has venido a la orilla" (HWB 229)

"Take my life" (HWB 389)

"Here I am, Lord" (HWB 395)

"How clear is our vocation, Lord" (HWB 541)

"Be thou my vision" (HWB 545)

"God the Spirit, Guide and Guardian" (HWB 632)

"Whom shall I send?"(HWB 633)

Scripture passages:

Exodus 3:1-12	Acts 6:1-7
Isaiah 6:1-8	Acts 13:1-2
Matthew 4:18-22	2 Timothy 1:3-7

Visual setting:

Encourage the use of visual symbols that speak of the person's call and commitment to ministry. These could include: a basin and towel, a quilt, flowers or plant, or a candle.

[L: In commending _____ for this ministry, will you also uphold him/her in it?

P: We will stand by _____ in her/his calling.]

Examination (the candidate and presider(s) stand together before the congregation)

_____, the church is the family of God, the body of Christ, and the temple of the Holy Spirit.

All baptized people are called to make Christ known as Savior and Lord,

and to share in the building up of the church and the renewing of the world.

Now you are called to work as a pastor, priest,
and teacher,
together with all who share in the
ministry of Christ.
It will be your task to proclaim by word and deed
the gospel of Jesus Christ,
and to fashion your life in accordance
with its precepts.
You are to love and serve the people among
whom you work,
[to live with them in mutual accountability],
caring alike for young and old, strong and
weak, rich and poor.
You are to preach, to declare God's forgiveness to
penitent sinners,
to pronounce God's blessing, to preside at
baptism, the Lord's Supper, and other
events.
In all that you do, you are to nourish Christ's
people from the riches of his grace,
and strengthen them to glorify God in
this life and in the life to come.

Q: Do you believe that you are truly called by
God and God's church to this ministry?
A: I believe I am so called.

Q: Will you accept the office of ministry entrusted to you by this ordination?
A: I will.

Q: Will you respect and be guided by the beliefs and practices of the Mennonite church [and the work of this congregation and conference]?

A: I will.

Q: Do you believe that the Holy Scriptures of the Old and New Testaments are the Word of God and contain all things necessary for salvation?

A: I do.

Q: Will you be faithful in the study of these Scriptures so that you may have the mind of Christ?

A: I will.

Q: Will you endeavor to minister so that the reconciling love of Christ may be known and received?

A: I will.

Q: Will you undertake to be a faithful pastor to all whom you are called to serve, laboring together with them and your fellow ministers to build up the family of God?

A: I will.

Q: Will you do your utmost to pattern your life [and that of your family] in accordance with

the teachings of Christ, so that you may be a
wholesome example?

A: I will.

Q: Will you persevere in prayer, both in public
and in private, asking God's grace, both for
yourself and for others, and offering all your
labors to God, through the mediation of Jesus
Christ, and in the sanctification of the Holy
Spirit?

A: I will.

L: May the Lord who has given you the will to
do these things give you the grace and power
to perform them.

Candidate: Amen.

[L: Sisters and brothers, do you accept your role
in setting apart _____ for ministerial
leadership?

Will you honor her/his calling and also your
own? *(pause)*

Will you search the Scriptures and pray with
her/him? *(pause)*

Will you speak the truth in love? *(pause)*

Will you join her/him in mission? *(pause)*

P: We will, by God's grace.]

Prayer of Consecration
(The candidate kneels and the presider lays hands on

her/him. Others join in the laying on of hands according to local custom.)

L: O God, in your love you sent us your Son, a servant.

He humbled himself for our sake and accepted death.

You raised him to unending life.

We give you thanks that you have called our sister/brother, _____, into your Son's ministry.

Grant _____ a root in your kingdom that is deep and true,

and courage to place radical trust in your power and goodness.

Send _____ your Holy Spirit's presence, gifts, and guidance.

Bless _____ with faithfulness in servant-hood.

Grant her/him grace to fulfill her/his calling, shower her/him with an abundance of faith, hope, and love in the name of the Father, the Son, and the Holy Spirit.

P: Amen.

*Anointing of the candidate may follow, using the resources in **Healing and Lament** and/or the following:*

L: Loving God, your Son was anointed by the Holy Spirit, not to be served but to serve.

Let your Spirit come down upon _____ in fullness.

Let _____ be a minister of your healing
    love.
Let this oil be a sign to _____ of your pres-
    ence and protection.
I/we anoint you for blessing in the name of
    the Father, Son, and Holy Spirit. Amen.

*The ordinand stands and is greeted with the holy kiss
and/or the right hand of fellowship, and these words:*
L: Receive this Bible.
    Feed the flock of Christ.
    Help them to hear and heed God's truth.
    Be a faithful steward of all God entrusts to
        you.[67]

ORDINATION FORM 2

Presentation
Today is a significant day for many persons,
    especially for _____ [for _____
    (spouse), for _____ (family),
    for _____ (congregation)] and for
    God's people in this community and across
    the church.
    Today we acknowledge and affirm what God
        has been doing in your life, _____,
        in the life of _____ (congregation),
        and in the life of God's people.
This is a day of celebration, consecration, and
    commitment as you are ordained by the
    power of the Holy Spirit to pastoral ministry

here in _____(congregation), within
this _____(conference)

and wherever God may call you within the
Mennonite church.

_____, God has been at work all through
your life, calling you to be a follower of Jesus.
You have responded to that call.

In recent years, God and the people of God have
affirmed your gifts of leadership and ministry
within the community of faith and in mission
to the world.

The year(s) for which you were licensed
was/were a time to test your inner call and
the call of God's people.

You grew in your understanding of pastoring and
in your sense of calling.

Today we celebrate a particular call of God's people to a particular ministry.

Examination

Q: _____, do you today renew your baptismal
vows of commitment to Jesus Christ as your
Lord and Savior,

who, through the Holy Spirit, baptizes
with water and with fire

and gives spiritual gifts to all for ministry?

A: I do, by God's grace.

Q: _____, do you accept the call of this faith
community as a call from God?

Do you commit yourself to this congregation
to be Christ's representative among them,

both unafraid to lead and willing to live
in mutual accountability with them?

A: I do, by the help of God.

Q: _____, do you promise to devote yourself to
prayer, Bible study and the spiritual disciplines
so that as you grow in God's Word and wisdom,
you may become an agent of mercy and justice?

A: I do, God being my guide.

Q: _____, will you by the power of the Holy
Spirit,

work with others [elders/deacons, congregational leadership] and members of
this congregation so that the body of
Christ might be spiritually equipped to
grow into the likeness of Jesus?

Will you commit yourself to support the
Mennonite church and the work of the
conference, maintaining an open spirit
which is ready to receive and give counsel
within the congregation as well as within
the conference?

A: I will, by the power of the Holy Spirit.

[Q: _____ (spouse), _____ (candidate) has
been called to serve as an ordained minister of _____ (congregation).

We also recognize that you have many gifts and
invite you to share them as a member here.

Pastoring is a calling, and consequently your
life will be greatly affected by the
covenant that _____ (candidate) is making to this congregation.

Will you encourage _____ (candidate) to use
his/her pastoral gifts, and will you support him/her as is mutually fitting in
Christ?

Spouse: I will.]

L: _____, we have heard your promises.
Now, on behalf of these, your brothers and
sisters here at _____ (congregation),
and on behalf of _____ (conference),
we ordain you as a minister of the gospel of
Jesus Christ and commit this congregation to
your spiritual care.

L (to congregation): Sisters and brothers,
do you accept your role in setting apart
_____ for ministerial leadership?

Will you honor her/his calling and also your
own? *(pause)*

Will you search the Scriptures and pray with
her/him? *(pause)*

Will you speak the truth in love? *(pause)*

Will you join her/him in mission? *(pause)*

P: We will, by God's grace.

Prayer of ordination
(The candidate kneels and the presider lays hands on her/him. Others join in the laying on of hands according to local custom.)

L: Lord of the church, look with favor on your servant, whom we now dedicate to Christ's ministry.

Send forth upon _____ the Holy Spirit that she/he may be strengthened by the gift of your grace to carry out faithfully the work of the ministry.

May _____ excel in every virtue: in love that is sincere, in concern for the sick and the poor, in unassuming authority, in self-discipline, and in holiness of life.

May _____'s conduct exemplify your commandments.

May she/he remain strong and steadfast in Christ, giving to the world the witness of a pure conscience.

May _____, in this life imitate your Son, who came, not to be served but to serve, and one day reign with him in heaven.

We ask this through our Lord Jesus Christ, who lives and reigns with you and the Holy Spirit, one God forever and ever.

P: Amen.

Presentation of the Bible with these words:

L: Receive the Gospel of Christ, whose herald you now are. Believe what you read, teach what you believe, and practice what you teach.

The ordinand is greeted with the kiss of peace and/or right hand of fellowship.[68]

Additional Resource

Litany of Blessing

Leaders: Blessed is she/he who believed that there would be a fulfillment of what was spoken to her/him by the Lord.

All: May your spirit rejoice in God who does great and marvelous things.

Man: May you speak with the voice of the voiceless, and give courage to those in despair.

All: May your spirit rejoice in God who does great and marvelous things.

Woman: May you feed the hungry of mind and heart, and send away satisfied those who are empty.

All: May your spirit rejoice in God who does great and marvelous things.

Woman: May you not be alone, but find support in your struggle, and sisters to rejoice with you.

All: May your spirit rejoice in God who does great and marvelous things.

Man: May your vision be fulfilled, in company with us; may you have brothers on your journey.

All: May your spirit rejoice in God who does great and marvelous things.

Leaders: Blessed is she/he who believed there would be a fulfillment of what was spoken to her/him by the Lord.

All: May your spirit rejoice in God who does great and marvelous things.[69]

INSTALLATION OF A MINISTER

The installation of a minister happens when someone who has been previously ordained in the
Mennonite church or whose ordination elsewhere
has been accepted by the Mennonite church is
then affirmed to ministry in a specific congregation, welcomed by it, and accepted as its leader. In
order for the wider church to participate in the act
of installation, it is suitable for it to be held on a
Sunday afternoon or evening. If the person being
installed is to preach in this service, the installation should precede the sermon; if another person
preaches, the installation appropriately follows
the sermon. If the installation happens immediately following ordination, it may be abbreviated in
any way that still preserves its goal, which is to set
forth clearly the mutual relationship between the
minister and this congregation.

Presentation

L: Sisters and brothers,
   we have gathered today in the presence of
   God and this assembly to install _____
   as pastor of this congregation.
   Who presents _____ for installation?

P: We present _____.
   Believing that we have been guided by the
   Spirit of God, we have called _____ to
   be our minister.

L: In commending _____ for this ministry, will

you also uphold _____ in it?

P: We will stand by _____ in her/his calling.

Examination (the candidate and presiders stand together before the congregation)

Q: Do you hold to the promises you made at your baptism and ordination?

A: I do.

Q: Do you believe that this calling and your acceptance of it are in response to the leading of the Holy Spirit?

A: I do.

Q: Will you seek to be faithful in prayer, in setting forth the Scriptures, and in seeking the good of this congregation?

A: I will.

Q: Will you seek to live honestly, openly, and justly with your brothers and sisters in this congregation?

A: I will.

L (to congregation): Sisters and brothers, you have heard the commitment to ministry in this congregation made by _____. Do you receive _____ as your minister? Will you seek to live honestly, openly, and justly with _____?

P: We will.

[Optional affirmation by fellow ministers in the congregation, either a co-pastor or members of a plural ministry: I/We affirm you as a/the leader of this congregation, and offer myself/ourselves as your partner(s) in ministry with it.]

Prayer of installation (the candidate remains standing)

L: O God, you call your people to service through the church.

Bless the covenant we have made together as pastor and people.

We thank you for the calling to ministry that comes to each of us.

On this day, we especially thank you for the calling to pastoral ministry.

Be a source of strength to _____,

endow her/him with the gifts of the Spirit: love, joy, peace, patience, kindness, goodness, faithfulness, gentleness, and self-control.

Bind us to one another in the bond of peace.

"Now may the God of peace,

who brought back from the dead our Lord Jesus, the great shepherd of the sheep,

by the blood of the eternal covenant, make you complete in everything good

so that you may do God's will, working among us that which is pleasing in God's sight,

through Jesus Christ, to whom be the glory forever and ever." (Heb. 13:20-21)

P: Amen.[70]

Licensing of a Minister toward Ordination

People are ready for licensing when they have followed the promptings of the Holy Spirit and the church to consider ordained ministry and when they have prepared themselves through prayer and study for a pastoral assignment. The service of licensing may be initiated by the candidate's home congregation, or by the congregation inviting him/her into ministry in their midst as part of an exploration of ongoing suitability for ordained ministry. Licensing is always for a specified time of testing, usually not less than one year and not more than two years during which the candidate and the calling congregation share in a process of discernment. Licensing belongs in the regular Sunday service, most appropriately after the sermon, whose theme should be mission and ministry.

Presentation

L: "When Jesus saw the crowds, he had compassion for them

because they were harassed and helpless, like sheep without a shepherd.

Then he said to his disciples, 'The harvest is plentiful but the laborers are few;

therefore ask the Lord of the harvest to send out laborers into his harvest.'"
(Mt. 9:36-38)

All who heed the call from the Lord of the harvest

and enter the covenant of baptism
become Christ's ministers.

All receive the Spirit; all are given gifts.

Through the Spirit, God continues to call
women and men to the gift of ordained
ministry.

Spiritual receptivity and practice in the day-
to-day tasks of ministry
are necessary to test and to reinforce
someone's sense of call.

We gather here today because we believe that
God is drawing _____ to ordained ministry.

The year(s) ahead will be a time of testing to
see if you, _____,
are willing and able to follow this path,
to see if this set-apart ministry is the one
to which God and the church are calling
you.

The congregation and conference have confirmed your emerging sense of calling,
and promise to join you in this time of
discernment.

As you faithfully pursue the purposes you
here affirm,
you will become more certain of God's
will for your life.

*Questions (the candidate and presider(s) stand togeth-
er before the congregation)*

Q: _____, do you renew your baptismal vow,

claiming Christ's grace, offering him your obedience?

A: I do.

Q: Is it your heart's desire to serve God according to God's will for you?

A: It is.

Q: Do you affirm your devotion to Christ's church and mission? Will you seek to grow in faithfulness to it, guided by the Holy Spirit and Scripture, in the company of this congregation and conference?

A: I will.

Q: Are you willing to accept this ministry as a stewardship of God's grace and as preparation for further service?

A: I am.

Prayer of blessing (the candidate remains standing)
L: Lord of creation, Lord of the church,
> we bless you for the gifts you give to all whom you have made,
> and which you call forth through your Spirit for the sake of the kingdom.

Thank you for _____, for your Spirit's work in _____'s life,
> for _____'s seeking of your will above all else.

Grant _____ a discerning heart, confidence
in your call,

> strength and joy in the tasks of
> ministry now set before her/him.

Make us partners with _____ in ministry,
constant in support,

> gentle in criticism, prayerful in all
> things.

We ask this in the name of Jesus, our Servant
and Master. Amen.

*The candidate is received with the holy kiss and/or the
right hand of fellowship.*

Declaration

L: _____, you are licensed to Christian ministry for this congregation

> in the name of the Father, the Son, and the
> Holy Spirit. Amen.

Preach the word, offer the ordinances, bear
witness in word and deed to the gospel.

"May the God of peace sanctify you entirely;
and may your spirit and soul and body be
kept sound and blameless

> at the coming of our Lord Jesus Christ.

The one who calls you is faithful, and will do
it." (1 Thess. 5:23-24)

P: Amen.[71]

LICENSING/COMMISSIONING FOR
SPECIFIC MINISTRY

Some people experience the call to ministry in highly specific terms. It comes to them through a particular time, place, or institution. They may not be ready for a lifetime of professional ministry, but they are prepared to take on a particular role in their present settting. Church work might not be their source of income, but it might well be part of their life vocation. Historically, the tradition of being a farmer and a minister is an honorable example. The pastoral role to which someone is called might be identified with a particular institution, like a school, but is not a full pastorate, missionary role, or chaplaincy. In all such cases, the church's support of the person and its affirmation of the person's spiritual gifts is crucial. The parts in square brackets may be omitted where the ministry is not in the context of a congregation.

Presentation

L: Brothers and sisters, we are gathered today in the presence of God and this assembly to commission _____ to ministry.

Who presents _____ for commissioning to ministry?

P: We present our sister/brother _____ to be set apart for the ministry of _____ in the world.

[L: In commending _____ for this ministry, will you also uphold him/her in it?

P: We will stand by _____ in his/her calling.]

Examination (the candidate and presider(s) stand together before the congregation)

_____, the church is the family of God, the body of Christ, and the temple of the Holy Spirit.

All baptized people are called to make Christ known as Savior and Lord,

and to share in the building up of the church and the renewing of the world.

Now you are called to work as (name the ministry), together with all who share in the ministry of Christ.

It will be your task to proclaim by word and deed the gospel of Jesus Christ,

and to fashion your life in accordance with its precepts.

You are to love and serve the people among whom you work, [to live with them in mutual accountability],

caring alike for young and old, strong and weak, rich and poor. *(The specific responsibilities of the person's ministry may be named here.)*

In all that you do, you are to nourish Christ's people from the riches of his grace,

and strengthen them to glorify God in this life and in the life to come.

Q: Do you believe that you are truly called by God and God's church to this ministry?

A: I believe I am so called.

Q: Will you respect and be guided by the beliefs and practices of the Mennonite church [and the work of this congregation and conference]?

A: I will.

Q: Do you believe that the Holy Scriptures of the Old and New Testaments are the Word of God and contain all things necessary for salvation?

A: I do.

Q: Will you be faithful in the study of these Scriptures so that you may have the mind of Christ?

A: I will.

Q: Will you endeavor to minister so that the reconciling love of Christ may be known and received?

A: I will.

Q: Will you do your utmost to pattern your life [and that of your family] in accordance with the teachings of Christ, so that you may be a wholesome example?

A: I will.

Q: Will you persevere in prayer, both in public and in private, asking God's grace, both for yourself and for others, and offering all your labors to God, through the mediation of Jesus Christ, and in the sanctification of the Holy Spirit?

A: I will.

L: May the Lord who has given you the will to do these things give you the grace and power to perform them.

P: Amen.

[L: Sisters and brothers, do you accept your role in setting apart _____ for leadership? Will you honor her/his calling and also your own? *(pause)* Will you search the Scriptures and pray with her/him? *(pause)* Will you speak the truth in love? *(pause)* Will you join her/him in mission? *(pause)*

P: We will, by God's grace.]

Prayer of commissioning (the candidate remains standing)

L: Holy God, your love for us was so great that Christ emptied himself of his equality with you, taking on the form of a slave.

Grant _____ the mind of Christ; grant him/her a share in Christ's ministry.

Pour out your Holy Spirit on _____ so that he/she might be given

all the gifts needed to be a faithful
minister.

Now may the God of peace who brought
back from the dead our Lord Jesus,
the great shepherd of the sheep, by
the blood of the eternal covenant,
make you complete in everything good,
so that you may do God's will,
working among us that which is
pleasing in God's sight, through
Jesus Christ,
to whom be the glory forever and ever.

P: Amen.

*The candidate is received with the holy kiss and/or the
right hand of fellowship.*

*The newly commissioned person may be given a Bible
if preaching is central to his/her ministry. Otherwise, a
gift symbolizing the focus of the ministry may be
given.*[72]

Commissioning of Deacons and Elders

The ancient and honorable office of deacon dates from apostolic days when deacons were appointed to represent the church in the care of the poor and needy (Acts 6:1-6). In the course of time, new duties were added to their role, making them more and more central to the life of the congregation (1 Tim. 3:8-13). The calling of deacons to "wait on tables" (Acts 6) soon took on a double meaning in that deacons assisted the presbyter in preparing and serving the Lord's Supper. To this was added their roles of presiding at footwashing and assisting at baptism. From the early church onward through the Reformation, deacons were assigned both practical duties of overseeing ministry to the poor and disadvantaged within and beyond the congregation, and the spiritual task of taking initiative to heal misunderstanding and strife in the congregation.

The diaconate was the one office in the early church clearly offered to women. This practice is attested to in Mennonite sources from the seventeenth through the nineteenth centuries. At the end of the nineteenth century, Mennonites in Germany, Russia, and the United States reinstituted the women's diaconate as an order of celibate women with ministries in health care and education. As communities, these celibates died out, but individual women and men have continued to believe themselves called to celibate diaconal and other ministries and have received formal or informal support from the church (see **Blessing of a Life of Celibacy**).

Many variations exist in the understanding and responsibilities of deacons. In some areas, only one deacon is chosen; in others, there is one deacon for every fifty or so members. Ordination for life was the norm until the 1960s; now deacons are often commissioned for a set time. In some settings, married partners are commissioned as a couple for service. Where this is the case, both should answer the questions and be prayed over together. In some circles, the role of deacon has been eliminated in recent decades because of strong associations with church discipline. Though in need of reform in recent times, the diaconate is a biblical office which identifies a set of gifts and needs in the life of the congregation and fosters the sharing of ministry.

In the New Testament church, elders or presbyters were appointed in some places as congregational leaders [Numbers 11:16-29; Acts 20:17-38; I Timothy 5:17-22; I Peter 5:1-5]. At the Reformation, Mennonites accepted an interpretation of the New Testament in which the elder was seen as the leading minister of a congregation or group of congregations. The terms "elder" and "bishop" were used interchangeably. Apart from rare references in subsequent Mennonite literature where an elder is described as someone with parallel responsibilities to those of deacons, this understanding of their role did not enter the Mennonite mainstream until the 1960s. Elders are now understood as women and men commissioned by the congregation for a set time, to share with the minister(s) spiritual oversight and pastoral care of the congregation.

The following order of commissioning may be used for setting aside deacons and elders because both share leadership of the congregation with the minister(s) for set times. But in most congregations, duties are complementary rather than identical. Exactly what each person is called to should be made clear to the candidate.

Presentation

L: Sisters and brothers, we have gathered here in the presence of God and this assembly to commission _____ as a deacon/elder in this congregation.

Who presents _____ for this commissioning?

P: We present _____ for the ministry of this congregation.

L: In commending _____ for ministry, will you also uphold _____?

P: We will stand by _____ in his/her calling.

Examination (the candidate and presider(s) stand together before the congregation)

Q: _____, do you renew your baptismal

vows, claiming Christ's grace, offering Christ
your obedience?

A: I do.

Q: Do you believe this calling and your acceptance of it to be in response to the leading of
the Holy Spirit?

A: I do.

Q: Will you trust in God's care,
        keep a discipline of prayer and Scripture
            study,
        strive to grow in love for those you serve,
        and seek to adorn the gospel you profess
            with a godly life?

A: I will.

L: Sisters and brothers, you have heard the com-
        mitment to ministry made by _____.
    Do you receive _____ as a deacon/elder
        in this congregation?

P: We do.

Commissioning (the candidate remains standing)

L: Holy God, your love for us was so great that
        Christ emptied himself of his equality
        with you, taking on the form of a slave.
    Grant _____ the mind of Christ; grant
        him/her a share in Christ's ministry.
    Pour out your Holy Spirit on _____ so that

_____ might be given all the gifts
needed to be a faithful deacon/elder.
"Now may the God of peace, who brought
back from the dead our Lord Jesus,
the great shepherd of the sheep, by
the blood of the eternal covenant,
make you complete in everything
good so that you may do God's will,
working among us that which is
pleasing in God's sight, through Jesus
Christ,
to whom be the glory forever and
ever." (Heb. 13:20-21)

P: Amen.

Declaration

L: _____, you are commissioned as a dea-
con/elder in this congregation
in the name of the Father, the Son, and the
Holy Spirit. Amen.
Receive and give counsel, help us grow in
mission, build the unity of the church,
speak the truth in love, be a person of
prayer and Scripture.

*The person is greeted with the holy kiss and/or the
right hand of fellowship.*[73]

Lament and Healing

Perhaps worship and pastoral care intersect most profoundly in the ceremonies of congregational life which express the church's ministry of healing. For Mennonites, these rituals have traditionally included funerals, anointing with oil (often reserved for extreme cases of physical illness), and (very rarely) a service of reconciliation after sin or conflict have separated a person or group from the church.

In 1995, we committed ourselves to a vision statement emphasizing healing and hope. Article 10, Note 3, of our *Confession of Faith* states that "the church is called to be a channel of God's healing, which may include anointing with oil."

Many congregations are recovering the ministry of healing as part of normal church life. We who minister now have an opportunity to resurrect old rituals for a whole array of new situations, and to invite God's Spirit to breathe new life into them, for our time. Two of the four historic functions of pastoral care are healing and reconciling. We are now recovering these functions as part of our priestly ministry, rather than exercising them only in private "counseling" settings. When we lead ceremonies which express the church's healing ministries, we will want to do so with quiet authority in a caring manner, undergirded by prayer and by solid biblical teaching.

Of course the most familiar ritual of healing we offer is the funeral or memorial service. At the time of death, this ceremony provides the means for family, friends, and church community to grieve and remember in a way that brings healing and comfort, while giving expression to our hope of eternal life through Christ's resurrection.

Increasingly, we have opportunity to offer services of anointing with oil and the laying on of hands for those who desire healing in body, mind, spirit, or relationships. Sometimes these services take place in private settings, such as a hospital room; at other times a number of persons might come forward for private prayer in the gathered community; at still other times the whole congregation may wish to gather around to invite God's healing for a specific person or situation.

Through the church's healing ministry, we bring the whole person or situation into harmony with the life-giving Spirit of God. Through prayer and confession, obstacles of anxiety, fear, guilt, or broken relationships that block healing can be removed.

When we exercise the healing ministry of the church, we acknowledge that God's healing happens both through and beyond the medical and therapeutic practices prevalent in our society. We acknowledge that we humans are complex beings in whom body, mind, and spirit work together for or against wholeness in ways we don't fully understand. To experience healing is to be restored to wholeness in body, mind, and/or spirit, and to find our place again within the community. We believe healing will happen, but we do not presume that God will bring it according to our assumptions. Instead, we remain open to wholeness in whatever forms it may come.

Jesus' ministry demonstrated an unmistakable concern for the wholeness of persons in body, mind, and spirit—healing narratives make up fully one-fifth of the Gospels! The healing which Jesus brought left people not just cured but "whole"—restored to God and to their faith community. Consistently, Jesus refused to divide people into neat categories of body, mind, and spirit. In healing narrative after healing narrative, he moved easily between those categories as he restored people to wholeness and to full participation in the community. Jesus' ministry of healing and making whole continued to manifest itself in the early church through the Acts of the Apostles. We are reclaiming this ministry of the church for our day.

We are also reclaiming the power of lament as a prelude to healing. In situations such as physical or sexual abuse, congregational tension, business failure, job loss, family breakup, or natural disaster, lament is often necessary before healing can begin. As the church revives this ancient practice, the writers of the Psalms are our teachers. The psalms of lament include (1) a direct complaint or lament, (2) a reaffirmation of God as our hope, and (3) thanks for God's goodness.

To lament is to bring our experiences of disorientation to God without cover-up—to acknowledge that we are at the desperate edge of personal, family, or congregational life, and that things are not as they ought to be. Sometimes we as ministers need to lead congregations in asking "My God, my God, why have you forsaken me? Why are you so far from helping me, from the words of my groaning?" (Ps. 22:1). Or "How long must I bear pain in my soul, and have sorrow in my heart all day long?... Consider and answer me, O Lord my God!" (Ps. 13:2-3). To enable a congregation to bring such deep distress to God is a profound priestly/pastoral function. Through such expressions, the congregation can acknowledge things as they are and begin to rekindle its hope in God, so that God's healing can flow even in the midst of impossible, immobilizing, totally unacceptable situations, leading us to give thanks for God's goodness.

In addition to rituals of healing and lament, rituals of closure are gaining wider use in our churches. Sometimes these rituals can celebrate reconciliation—as when a broken relationship between persons or factions has been restored. At other times (divorce, congregational split, the conclusion of a process regarding abuse), rituals help us acknowledge that people have not been able to come back together, and healing is happening in other ways. When we as ministers lead services of closure, we do so respecting that for some the events are far from "finished." Yet it is an important priestly/pastoral function to acknowledge that we have come to this place and to invite God to lead us into deeper levels of healing.

MINISTRY AT THE TIME OF DEATH

The origins of funeral practices are lost in the furthest mists of human history. They are unlike some of the other rites of the church precisely because of their universal nature. People do them first of all because they are human. It is important for Christians to be aware of the universal dimensions of funeral practices, out of sensitivity to the basic needs, conscious and unconscious, which mourners bring, and so they can identify the insights and interpretations which Christian faith brings to bear on the reality of death and the experience of bereavement.

A Christian attitude to death is inseparable from the biblical accounts of the resurrection of Jesus Christ and his followers' experience of the saving power of his renewed presence. The fourth Gospel sees the whole of Jesus' ministry as an expression of glory in which death itself is an act of triumph. The cry of abandonment in Matthew and Mark and of resignation in Luke reflect another perception of Jesus' experience of death.

It is entirely fitting that Christian funerals reflect these various dimensions of the experience of death. Expressions of faith and hope in the face of death should leave room for the sense of anxiety and loss. They should enable the grief process. On the other hand, Christian funerals should not become unrelieved expressions of anguish and despair: there is a time for thanksgiving even in the midst of mourning.

Christian funerals have been shaped over the centuries by a variey of notions of what happens to those who have died. In earlier centuries, the idea of solidarity was paramount: the church was a single body moving toward an ultimate destiny which neither living nor dead had yet experienced. This view of things gradually gave way to a more individualistic preoccupation with immediate personal destiny.

When Christians gather in the face of death, we do so in the, sometimes trembling, faith that God's love for all God has created is steadfast. God's love overcame the power of evil, sin, and death in the resurrection of Jesus (1 Cor. 15). When believers die, they are hidden with Christ in God (Col. 3:3), awaiting the redemption of their bodies and of all creation (Rom. 8:18-25). We dare to hope in the wideness of God's mercy and so place no one outside its pale. But in the case of those who did not confess Christ, we do well to commend them to God's mercy without making specific claims, which in some cases, might violate their own beliefs. The portions of the funeral service in square brackets provide for this concern.

In a funeral or memorial service, we seek the presence of God in our grieving and give thanks for the life of the person who has died in the light of God's grace in Christ. God's grace is the center and circumference of the service. This comes to expression in the singing of hymns, prayer, Scripture reading, and preaching. An obituary and other reflections on the person's life should be included in this spirit. We gather not because of the accomplishments of the deceased (or the lack thereof) but because he/she was "a sinner of your saving, a lamb in your keeping." Except for extenuating circumstances, it is important that the service be held in the place where the person who has died worshipped.

It has been longstanding tradition for the whole Christian church to hold that miscarriages and stillbirths are not deaths because the person has not lived outside the womb. Many people across denominational lines now emphasize that this position withholds crucial liturgical and pastoral resources from grieving families. More and more families request private or public services to help them in their grief, and to commend to God a life that has been lost. Every life is equally precious to God, but the character of a service for someone who has lived longer and developed associations in the world will be different from that of a service for one who has not. A service in the home, a commemoration as part of a Sunday service, or a service unto itself is possible. Current practice is generally for the hospital to cremate the remains of a miscarriage and for the remains of a stillbirth to be buried.

The death of an infant and that of a small child leave us particularly bereft, the former because the life of the person ended before it could begin, the latter because a life was taken after the most intimate of attachments was already in place. The death of a small child calls for unusual tenderness without giving in to sentimentality. Even though the service may be simplified according to pastoral discretion, the proclamation of the steadfast love of God through the various elements of the service is no less important. All the parts in square brackets may be freely used because we believe that all children are included in the atoning work of Christ.

In times past, cremation was sometimes practiced by people who denied the possibility of eternal life with God and used the burning of the body to make this point. This is generally not the case today. Where cremation affirms the belief in the resurrection of the dead, it is an acceptable way of honoring someone's remains. Since we are creatures of flesh and blood, most of us need visible and tangible actions to complete inner experiences. Therefore, the actions of grieving and giving thanks, of releasing the person who has died to God, are most complete when cremation occurs in time for the urn to be present for the funeral.

Local customs vary as regards the viewing of the person who has died. Viewing may take place in a funeral parlor, church, or home. Depending on the size of the deceased's community, the viewing may go on from one to three days. It is a valuable time not only for those most immediately affected but for a person's wider circle of associates to grieve, give thanks, and release. It is good to begin or end the viewing with a devotional for the immediate family and friends.

Simplicity and modesty in the selection of a coffin and the presence of flowers is liberating. By encouraging it and suggesting how to be simple with dignity, the minister can free the bereaved from being intimidated by others' expectations and from trying to compensate for unresolved failures and alienations with outward show. Pastoral sensitivity to these realities at the time of death is crucial. Membership in a burial society helps prepare people to make wise choices.

Hymns:
"In thee is gladness" (HWB 114)
"The King of love my shepherd is" (HWB 170)
"Lift your glad voices" (HWB 275)
"Come, come, ye saints" (HWB 425)
"Shepherd me, O God" (HWB 519)
"Take thou my hand, O Father" (HWB 581)

"Children of the heavenly Father" (HWB 616)
"For all the saints" (HWB 636)

(See also HWB 63, 65, 69, 70, 75, 85, 86, 121, 133, 143, 146, 149, 169-171, 247, 250, 252, 259-283, 327-332, 336-339, 343, 355, 430, 443, 479, 481-486, 493, 497, 500, 518, 524, 526-530, 550-619)

Scripture passages:

Numbers 6:24-26	John 11:25-26
Deuteronomy 33:27	John 14:1-3
Psalm 16:9-11	Romans 8:18-23, 31-39
Psalm 23	Romans 14:7-9
Psalm 90:1-4, 15-16	1 Corinthians 15:20-22,
Psalm 103:1-4, 10-17	42-44a, 47-49, 51-57
Psalm 121	Philippians 3:7-11
Matthew 5:4	Philippians 4:7
Matthew 10:29-31	1 Thessalonians 4:13-14
Matthew 28:5-7a	1 Thessalonians 5:9-10
Mark 15:33-34	2 Timothy 4:6-8
Luke 2:29-32	1 Peter 1:3-5
John 6:48-51	Revelation 7:13-17
	Revelation 14:13

Visual setting:

Flowers are the usual visual element of a funeral or memorial service. Consider flower bulbs at an autumn funeral. A table with remembrances of the life of the deceased may be prepared for the viewing or the funeral. In addition to the obituary, consider reading appropriate excerpts from the deceased person's journal.

Prayers with a Person Who Is Dying
Scripture passages and hymns can be meaningfully prayed with and for the person.

(a)
Lord Jesus,
My only Savior, my Eternal Friend,
I know that I belong to you in life and death.
Hold me fast; receive me to yourself. Amen.

(b)
God of mercy,
into whose hands your Son Jesus Christ
commended his spirit at his last hour,
into those same hands
we now commend your servant _____,
that death may be for him/her the gate to life
and to eternal fellowship with you;
through Jesus Christ our Lord. Amen.[74]

Prayer with the Bereaved
This is appropriate immediately after death and/or at the beginning and end of the viewing.

Loving and merciful God,
we entrust our brother/sister, _____, to your
    mercy.
You loved him/her greatly in this life;
now that he/she is freed from all its cares,
give him/her fullness of joy in your presence.

The old order has passed away;
welcome _____ now into paradise
where there will be no more sorrow,
no more weeping or pain,
but only peace and joy
with Jesus, your Son,
and the Holy Spirit,
for ever and ever. Amen.[75]

Prayer at the Announcement of Death and Funeral Arrangements in Church

It is appropriate that a hymn accompany the announcement.

Lord, you have been our dwelling place in all
    generations.
Before the mountains were brought forth or ever
    you had formed the earth,
from everlasting to everlasting you are God.
We grieve the [untimely] death of our
    sister/brother.
[_____ was a sinner of your saving, a lamb in
    your keeping.]
We commend _____ to your eternal care, believ-
    ing that the passion of Jesus was also for
    _____.
Comfort us and all who knew _____ with the
    presence of your Holy Spirit.
For Jesus' sake. Amen.

THE FUNERAL

Silence or music
Hymn (during which the mourners, and if desired, the
coffin may enter)
Scripture sentences (such as Psalm 90:1-2; John 14:1-
3; 1 Corinthians 15:20-22)

Greeting
The peace of God which passes all understanding
keep our hearts and minds in Christ Jesus. Amen.
We have gathered here to thank God for the life
of our brother/sister, _____, to find comfort in
time of need, and to place ourselves in the presence of God whose love knows no end, in time or
eternity.

Opening Prayer
Lord, our God, you are great, eternal, and utterly
    to be trusted.
You give life to all of us.
Give us now your Spirit of comfort and hope.
Set our hearts at peace
so that we may bring our thanks and needs
    before you without fear.
In the strong name of Jesus Christ. Amen.

Obituary (in addition to or instead of this, there may
    be remembrances later in the service)
Hymn
Scripture

Sermon

Silence

Remembrances by family and friends
(Brevity is appropriate. Longer, more informal recollec-
tions are appropriate for the gathering after the service.)

Prayer of Thanksgiving and Petition
Sovereign God, with your whole church we offer
   you thanks
for all you have done for humanity through Jesus
   Christ.
By giving Jesus to live and die for us
you have disclosed your gracious plan for the
   world
and shown that your love has no limit.
By raising Christ from the dead you have
   promised that those
who trust in him will share his resurrection life.
For the assurance and hope of our faith
and for the saints who you have received into
   your eternal joy
our hearts cry out in thanks.
Now we lift up our hearts in gratitude for the life
   of _____,
now gone from among us,
      for all your goodness to him/her through
         many seasons,
      for all that he/she was to those who loved
         him/her,

and for everything in his/her life that reflect-
ed your goodness.
[We bless you that his/her sins are forgiven,
that suffering and bitterness are past,
that he/she is safe in your presence.]
Help us to release him/her to you, gracious God;
[assure us that in your keeping he/she is secure.]
Surround us and all who mourn today with your
unending compassion.
Do not let grief overwhelm your children or be
unending
or turn them against you.
Guide us on the course of our journey;
Help us so to live that we might not be ashamed
when we meet you on the last day.
Bring us in the company of all the redeemed to
your eternal kingdom,
through our Lord Jesus Christ. Amen.

Announcements

*Commendation of the one who has died to God (the
presider may stand beside the coffin or urn)*
Into your hands, eternal God, we commend [your
servant] _____. [Receive unto yourself, we
humbly ask, a sheep of your fold, a lamb of your
flock, a sinner of your redeeming.] Receive
_____ into the arms of your mercy, [into the company of your saints, into everlasting peace]. Amen.

Blessing of the congregation
The grace of our Lord Jesus Christ, the love of God, and the communion of the Holy Spirit be with us all. Amen.

Hymn
Music

The Committal

The same service is appropriate for burial or cremation, if the ashes are to be buried. This service may precede as well as follow the funeral.

The mourners gather around the grave.

Scripture sentences
(Hymn)
Prayer
In the midst of life, we are surrounded by death. With whom can we find refuge? Only with you, Lord God. Do not let us be the prey of death, but grant us eternal life through your Son's death and resurrection. In his strong name we pray. Amen.[76]

Committal
Seeing that the earthly life of [our brother/sister],
      _____, has come to an end,
    we commit his/her body to be buried,
    earth to earth, ashes to ashes, dust to dust,
    [confident of the resurrection to eternal life
    through our Lord Jesus Christ].

(The body is lowered into the grave, where possible.)

_____, may God bless you and keep you;
May the very face of God shine upon you,
    and be gracious to you.
May God's presence embrace you
    and give you peace. Amen.

(Some or all of the earth is shoveled into the grave, where possible.)

[For us this is the end, for _____ the beginning. Therefore, let us not grieve as those who have no hope.

"God has destined us not for wrath but for obtaining salvation through our Lord Jesus Christ, who died for us, so that whether we are awake or asleep we may live with Christ. Therefore encourage one another." (1 Thess. 5:9)]

Blessing
Now may the God of peace who brought back
    from the dead our Lord Jesus,
        the great shepherd of the sheep, by the
            blood of the eternal covenant,
        make you complete in everything good,
            so that you may do God's will,
        working among us that which is pleasing
            in God's sight, through Jesus Christ,

to whom be the glory forever and ever.
Amen. Go in peace.

Alternate prayer of commendation or committal

L: Give rest, O God, to your servant with your
saints,

> where sorrow and pain are no more,
> neither sighing, but life everlasting.

Creator and Maker of humankind, you only
are immortal,

> and we are mortal, formed of the earth,
> and to the earth we shall return:

> for so you did ordain when you creat-
> ed us, saying,

> Dust thou art and unto dust thou
> shalt return.

P: All we go down to the dust, and, weeping,
over the grave, we make our song:

> Alleluia, alleluia, alleluia.

Give rest, O Christ, to your servant with your
saints,

> where sorrow and pain are no more,
> neither sighing, but life everlast-
> ing. Amen.[77]

MEMORIAL SERVICE FOR AN INDIVIDUAL

The memorial service presupposes a Christian service
of burial or cremation. This may be a committal service in the same location, or a funeral service in one
location followed by a memorial service in another
one; e.g., if the deceased had lived in different parts of

the country or world. The order of the service can be almost the same as that of a funeral, but the spirit is different: the hard task of burying the person is past, and the mourners can slowly begin to offer thanks for the person's life. The hymns, prayers, Scripture readings, and sermon should reflect that fact but should not try to escape the fact of death. A longer period for reflecting on the meaning of the person's life is appropriate, but it should not replace the sermon so that the comforts of Scripture and the grace of God in the person's life is the centerpiece of the service.

Opening Prayer
Eternal God, we praise you that in you we live and move and have our being.
We thank you for the unending life offered to us in Jesus Christ,
> through his death on the cross and your raising him to life again.
We thank you for the life of _____ and all that he/she meant to us;
> for those things in his/her life which gave us glimpses of your goodness and love.
Help us to release him/her to you, that our grief may neither be overwhelming nor unending.
Assure us of your love, strengthen our trust in your grace, and grant us your peace,
> through Jesus Christ our Lord. Amen.[78]

Prayer of Thanksgiving and Petition

Bountiful God, source of life, beyond knowledge
and thought, mysterious and profound:

> we thank you because we have seen you
> in _____.

We thank you for your life in him/her with all its
risks and commitments,

> and for your love given and received by
> him/her among family and friends;
> for [*share thoughts appropriate to the life of
> the departed*].

We sorrow at his/her passing because we were
enriched by his/her presence.

Help us through his/her death to see more
deeply into the meaning of his/her life and
our own,

> and to grasp more firmly the hope that
> life is longer than our years and the
> love you have shown us in Christ is
> stronger than death,
> through Jesus Christ our Lord. Amen.[79]

MEMORIAL SERVICE FOR A PUBLIC TRAGEDY

On such an occasion, a public expression of grief
allows those who have been affected to mark the
occasion collectively and to know that what they
have been through has not gone unnoticed.

A memorial service is not a funeral. Funerals
are personal and relate more immediately to the
release of the body. A memorial service is part of
the reflective and healing process. Survivors need

time to recover physically, so the service may be three, six, or even twelve months after the event.

Preparation should involve consultation with the bereaved. Representatives of the community may be invited to take part. The names of those who have died should be mentioned at some point or written in the order of service. Onlookers and those who helped in a rescue should not be overlooked as they too have been affected and need to feel a part of what is being expressed. All this underlines the fact that such a service will need to be specially planned and involve wide consultation.

DEATH OF AN INFANT OR CHILD
(may also be appropriate in the case of a miscarriage or stillbirth)

(a)
Merciful God, healer of broken hearts,
> we ask you to look in pity and compassion upon your servants
> whose joy has been turned into mourning.
Comfort them and grant that they may be drawn closer together by their common sorrow.
Dwell with them and be their refuge through Jesus Christ our Lord. Amen.[80]

(b)
Almighty God, you make nothing in vain, and love all that you have made.

Comfort these parents in their sorrow, and console
  them by the knowledge of your unfailing love;
through Jesus Christ our Lord. Amen.[81]

A Sudden or Violent Death

(a)
"As a mother comforts her child, so I will comfort
  you," says the Lord.
      We entrust _____ into your hands,
      knowing that you alone are the one to
      satisfy the longings of his/her heart.
Lord, you are the one who brings good out of evil,
      so now we pray that you might bring
      something good out of _____'s
      tragic death.
We pray for all those touched by _____'s life
  and death.
Help us to hear what you are saying to us.
Turn us away from all that we know to be wrong.
Help us to show love and understanding to those
  around us.
Forgive us for any ways in which we may have
  hurt _____.
God of compassion, you know us better than we
  know ourselves.
Bind the wounds of our sorrow and surround us
  with your love,
      through Jesus Christ our Lord. Amen.[82]

(b)
Almighty God,

we know that we should forgive those
who have so defied the way of love and
justice,

but the pain and the anger seem too great
to do so.

For now, we ask you to do for us what we cannot
do for ourselves:

forgive those who have committed this
crime and heal that which is flawed in
them.

We also pray that you will help us to forgive,

that we may be set free from bitterness
and know your peace,

through Jesus Christ our Lord. Amen.[83]

(c)

Lord Jesus Christ, you spoke of your Father's
love for all people;

help us to know that your love will never
be withdrawn from _____ or from us.

Lord Jesus Christ, you wrestled with questions of
life and death in Gethsemane;

help us to know that you understand and
are present where there is anguish of
mind.

Lord Jesus Christ, you gave hope beyond death to
a dying man on a cross;

help us to know that you did not withdraw hope from _____.

Lord Jesus Christ, we pray for ourselves and for
all who are bereft at this time,

knowing that in you we have a high
priest who sympathizes with our weaknesses.

Bring us now to the throne of grace that we may
receive mercy to help in time of need. Amen.[84]

CONFESSION AT THE TIME OF DEATH

God of mercy, our love is imperfect and our
friendship is unreliable;

forgive us for the failings of our relationships
with _____.

For leaving things unsaid, forgive us.

For speaking too soon, forgive us.

For opportunities missed, forgive us.

For things we did that were better left undone,
forgive us.

For love we lacked, and love we hid, forgive us.

Eternal God,

By your love which does not fail and now holds
_____ secure,

cover our faults, renew and remake us, and guide
us in

all the future until we come, with _____,
into the joy and unity

of your presence, through Jesus Christ our Lord.
Amen.[85]

MEMORIAL PRAYERS

These prayers are suitable for an annual remembrance of deaths; Eternity Sunday, the Sunday
before Advent, is an especially appropriate occa-

sion for remembering and giving thanks for those who have died.

(a)
HWB 801, 802, 805

(b)
Bring us, O Lord God
at our last awakening
    into the house and gate of heaven
to enter into that gate
    and dwell in that house
where there shall be no darkness
    nor dazzling,
but one equal light
no noise nor silence but one equal music
no fears nor hopes but one equal possession
no ends nor beginnings but one equal eternity;
in the habitation of thy glory and dominion,
world without end. Amen.[86]

(c)
Compassionate God,
    you who made us, whose love will not let
        us go,
    have brought us to the end of another year
        of grace.
Thank you for the people whose lives we have
    shared this year.
We mourn our separation from those who have
    died, yet not without hope.

We groan with all creation for our redemption,
for the coming of your kingdom.
We wait for Christ to return to complete your
work with us.
Give us grace to wait for him patiently, passion-
ately, doing his deeds.
Even so, come Lord Jesus. Amen.

ANOINTING WITH OIL

An important part of the spiritual renewal of the
twentieth century is the recovery of the healing
ministry to the normal life of the church. Healing
not only involves the mending of the body but
also brings the whole person into harmony with
the life-giving Spirit of God.

Jesus announced the good news of the kingdom in three ways—preaching, teaching, and
healing. Jesus passed this threefold ministry on to
the disciples and their followers. Healing is one of
the endowments of the Spirit mentioned in lists of
spiritual gifts in the New Testament (e.g., 1 Cor.
12). The church's ministry of personal healing is
woven from the same cloth as its work for peace,
justice, and healing of corporate brokenness.

Services of healing need proper preparation. It
is important that persons receiving this ministry
perceive it as a way of committing themselves and
their affliction to the Lord rather than as a guarantee of their physical recovery or as a replacement
for medical care. The focus of such services should

be upon God, and God's resources for making people whole. It is God who heals. The support of the caring community, the love expressed through such services, and the meditation on God's goodness almost always bring a healing of spirit or attitude apart from any physical healing. Physical healing sometimes follows because of the peace of spirit and climate of love.

The laying on of hands and anointing are historic symbolic acts claiming the person for God's kingdom and rule. Anointing in the Bible was used in the consecration of leaders—for empowerment (Isa. 61:1), to convey a spirit of gladness (Heb. 1:9), as medicine or cleansing, and as a symbol of the Holy Spirit. The disciples of Jesus used oil in anointing the sick (Mk. 6:13), and the early church continued this practice (Jas. 5:14-15). Anointing with oil is not something magical, but is a tangible way of speaking to the sick person of the love of Christ, the presence of the Holy Spirit, and the solidarity of the congregation.

Through the centuries, anointing moved from its original intention of healing and a claim on God's presence to last rites for dying persons. Across the denominational spectrum, this narrowing of the meaning of anointing is being broadened. The increased use of oil in cooking, hygiene, and health care has helped to make oil a meaningful sign of healing in our time.

The post-apostolic church anointed on various

occasions, such as baptism and ordination, to over-come lust and to foster surrender to the purposes of God. References in post-sixteenth-century Mennonite and Baptist literature refer to anointing for healing. Early in this century, anointing was list-ed as an ordinance in Daniel Kaufman's influential Mennonite theology. Anointing seems to have been practiced by all Mennonite groups for seriously ill people who sought recovery from their sickness. It was usually held in home or hospital, with a minis-ter and deacon present with the stricken person's family, sometimes together with the Lord's Supper. In the liturgical reforms of the present generation, anointing for healing has also been offered as a pub-lic service, either unto itself or as part of another ser-vice, often in conjunction with the Lord's Supper.

Anointing can be meaningful:
- in a decline in health, suffering from a disease, an injury, emotional illness
- before scheduled surgery
- before making a weighty decision
- when one has received word of a terminal illness
- when requested for someone unable to speak for him/herself; e.g., a young child or uncon-scious person
- when there is a fracture of relationships

Pastoral judgment is necessary to decide whether anointing belongs in a public or private set-ting. When someone is suffering great physical or emotional pain, a private setting offers more serenity. In situations where the person is infirm, he or she is probably not able to participate in a public service.

In a private service, the focus is on one individual, in the company of a few family and friends. All the elements of the service apply in a deeply personal way. In a public service that is not the regular Sunday assembly of the congregation, the private service may be adapted for a congregation and a number of individuals seeking healing on the same occasion. When the offer of anointing is included in the regular Sunday assembly, it may come at the beginning or end of communion. The intense and intimate atmosphere of the Lord's Supper provides a meaningful setting for anointing. Here individuals come forward during congregational singing or worship music and speak their desire to the minister, on the basis of which follows the "laying on of hands" formula of the private service.

The relationship between sin and sickness is mysterious and cannot be reduced to a matter of cause and effect. We do know that unconfessed hurt and sin and the incapacity to forgive affect a person's health. Without pressing this point, people seeking anointing should be invited to confess their sins. Where anointing is part of the Lord's Supper, a general confession of sin by the congregation might serve such individuals' need. Also, the *Questions to the person to be anointed* could be printed in the bulletin as an aid to inward preparation for anointing.

Olive oil is the traditional oil used in anointing. It or another oil is placed in a small container. A hint of scent may be added if there are no known allergies. It may be held or placed on the Lord's Table so that the minister may dip a finger into it and make the sign of the cross when the Trinity is invoked.

Hymns:
"There's a wideness in God's mercy" (HWB 145)
"O healing river" (HWB 372)
"Healer of our every ill" (HWB 377)
"By Peter's house" (HWB 378)
"O Christ, the healer" (HWB 379)
"Come, ye disconsolate" (HWB 497)
"Oh, have you not heard" (HWB 606)
"There is a balm in Gilead" (HWB 627)
(See also HWB 627-631)

Scripture passages:

Psalm 23	Matthew 11:25-30
Psalm 25	Mark 5:21-43
Psalm 42	Mark 6:12-13
Psalm 90	Luke 18:35-43
Psalm 91	Romans 8
Psalm 103:1-13	James 5:13-18
Psalm 130	

Visual setting:
Symbols of light—candles, oil lamp—represent the presence of Christ. Displaying a flask of oil helps draw attention to the significance of the event.

Private Anointing of the Sick

(may be adapted to other kinds of anointing, as listed above)

Hymn

Introduction

"Are any among you suffering? They should pray.... Are any among you sick? They should call for the elders of the church and have them pray over them, anointing them with oil in the name of the Lord." (Jas. 5:13-14)

Welcome

Opening Prayer

All: O God of peace,

you teach us that in returning and rest we shall be saved,

in quietness and confidence shall be our strength.

By the might of your Spirit lift us, we pray,

into your presence that we may be still and know that you are God,

through Jesus our Lord. Amen.[87]

Scriptures

Confession of Sin

All: "Have mercy on me, O God, according to your steadfast love; according to your abundant mercy blot out my transgressions. Create in me a clean heart, O God, and put a new and right spirit within me." (Ps. 51:1,10)

(silence)

L: The Lord has put away all our sin. God's mercy is from everlasting to everlasting.

P: Amen.

Questions to the person to be anointed

Q: _____, is it your heart's desire to place your life in God's hands in life and death?

A: Yes, it is.

Q: Have you asked for Christ's forgiving, healing presence in all your weaknesses and sins?

A: Yes, I have.

Q: Have you accepted the witness of God's Spirit with your spirit that you are a child of God?

A: Yes, I have.

[Single question for those unable to respond to the above:

Q: Do you trust that the Lord Jesus will care for you, whatever happens?

A: Yes, I do.]

Private exchange of concerns between minister and person

Laying on of hands

L: _____, I lay my hands on you in the name
      of Jesus, beseeching him to uphold you
      and fill you with his grace that you may
      know the power of his love.[88]

*Free prayer based on the concerns expressed by the sick
person and those with him/her (by leader and people,
as appropriate)*

L (as the oil is applied): I anoint you with oil for
      healing of mind, body, and spirit in the name
      of the Father, the Son, and the Holy Spirt.
      Amen.

Closing
L: "What then are we to say about these things?
      If God is for us who is against us?
      The One who did not withhold his own Son,
            but gave him up for all of us,
                  will he not with him also give us
                  everything else?
P: For I am convinced that neither death, nor
      life, … nor anything in all creation,
                  will be able to separate us from the
                  love of God in Christ Jesus our
                  Lord." (Rom. 8:31, 38)
L (with hands on the anointed person): And now
      to God
                  who by the power that is at work
                  within us
                  is able to do far more abundantly than
                  we can ask or imagine,

to God be glory in the Church and in
Christ Jesus,
to all generations, forever and ever.
Amen.

_____, may God bless you and keep you;
May the very face of God shine upon you,
and be gracious to you.
May God's presence embrace you
and give you peace. Amen.
P: Amen.

Hymn

Anointing After Divorce

To be alive is to know the possibility of pain. Our
sister/brother has come to know the pain of separation, of alienation. We believe that God wills for
us health of mind, of body, of human relationships. We believe, too, that all healing has its
source in God. Living in this faith, we claim the
divine promise of healing for our sister/brother.

_____, you are anointed for repentance, rec-
ognizing that all of us have known and con-
tributed to brokenness.

_____, you are anointed for faith, that your
trust in God's love and power may be confirmed
and strengthened.

_____, you are anointed for healing, that you may be restored to the wholeness of being that God wills for all who have experienced pain.[89]

Additional Prayers for Anointing
(adaptable to other occasions of need)

(a)

_____, I anoint you with oil in the name of our
    Lord Jesus Christ.
May our heavenly Father make you whole in
    body and mind,
        and grant you the inward anointing of his
            Holy Spirit,
        the Spirit of strength and joy and peace.
        Amen.

(b)

As you are outwardly anointed with this holy oil,
        so may the God of grace grant you the
            inward anointing of the Holy Spirit.
Of his great mercy may God forgive you your
    sins,
        release you from suffering,
        and restore you to wholeness and
            strength.
May God deliver you from all evil,
        preserve you in all goodness,
        and bring you to everlasting life, through
            Jesus Christ our Lord. Amen.

(c)

_____, may Christ, the Light of the world,
    drive away from you all darkness and all
        assaults of evil.
In the name of God, Father, Son, and Holy Spirit,
    I lay my hands upon you:
        may God fill you with healing, light, and
            peace. Amen.

(d)

_____, I anoint you with oil in the name of the
    Father, and of the Son, and of the Holy Spirit.
O God of all comfort, our help in time of need,
    we humbly ask you to visit and heal your
        servant, _____.
Look upon him/her with the assurance of your
    care and goodness;
        save him/her from temptation and
            despair,
        and give him/her patience under afflic-
            tion and enable him/her to live
                the remainder of life in wholeness.

(*then addressing the person, say:*)
May your weakness be turned to strength,
    your sorrow to joy,
    your illness to wholeness, harmony, and
        peace,
    as you commit your body, mind, and spir-
        it into the care of our Lord. Amen.

(e)

God of our life and source of our salvation,
we gather around our brother/sister
_____,
to pray for your healing work to begin in
him/her.
Send your comforting Spirit to renew his/her
strength.
Save him/her from despair. Take from him/her
fear of the unknown.
Free him/her from hatred, shame, or guilt.
Protect _____ from the evils that would
destroy faith in you.
Open his/her heart to receive your peace.
Bring relief to suffering.
Hold him/her in your fierce love.
May _____ know the healing presence of
Christ through the touch of all who minister
to him/her.
We trust your power to bring life out of death,
light out of darkness, and hope out of despair.
Amen.[90]

Congregational Discernment

Decision making in the congregation. How realistic is it? Are we adequately equipped to do it? Or is this simply a matter of one person's opinion pitted against another? Why is it that we often feel these can be some of the least holy moments in the life of the church? Because the situations and emotions involved in discernment and discipline are much more conflicted than is the case with baptism or communion, we shrink from trying to find a public way of carrying out discernment and discipline.

Confession of Faith in a Mennonite Perspective emphasizes the importance of discernment in the Christian life. In at least three separate articles, it calls attention to this important task. Article 14 states, "According to the teaching of Jesus Christ and the apostles, all believers participate in the church's mutual care and discipline as appropriate. Jesus gave the church authority to discern right and wrong and to forgive sins when there is repentance or to retain sins when there is no repentance. When becoming members of the church, believers therefore commit themselves to give and receive counsel within the faith community on important matters of doctrine and conduct."

With respect to calling leadership to serve the church, discernment is again recognized in Article 15 as a responsibility of the congregation.

Article 16 speaks of the decision-making process both within congregations and among congregations in conference settings, as well as in larger church bodies. It offers consensus as a way of coming to unity in the church. Consensus is described as "when the church has come to one mind on the matter, or when those who dissent have indicated that they do not wish to stand in the way of a group decision. Consensus does not necessarily mean complete unanimity."

Yet all of this begs the questions, "Where do we go for help in understanding what discernment is and how to do it in the church?" As a Christian tradition that is committed to following God's Word and Jesus' teachings, we Mennonites believe the Bible must be our primary source. But how are we to use the Bible in decision making? We acknowledge that we do not read or understand the Bible in a vacuum, but through a tradition that has come to us. We must acknowledge that process and accept it, always remaining open to critiquing it as appropriate.

Additionally, Scripture does not always offer direct teaching on many of the problems we face today (e.g., if and for how long to continue extraordinary treatment for someone in terminal stages of dying, what is a just wage to pay employees, what is the appropriate percentage for a pastoral recall). Nevertheless, the Bible is the authoritative source for guiding our decisions.

We acknowledge that the Holy Spirit (Jn. 16:7) helps us understand the Bible more fully. Like the disciples on the road to Emmaus, an encounter with the risen Christ can open our eyes to truly understand the biblical narrative. There is a continual process of comprehension involved in discernment. This is what Paul means when he speaks of the "renewing of your mind."

The matter is complicated by the reality that on some issues, the Bible may offer a range of options rather than one definitive word. While Matthew 7:1 tells us "Do not judge, so that you may not be judged," the apostle Paul seems to encourage the Christians in the communities where he established congregations to practice prudent discernment. Were Jesus, as Matthew recorded his words, and Paul talking about the same thing? Or are judgment and discernment sometimes different?

The Greek word "krino" is used for "judgment" in the Matthew text. It often refers to the sense of decision making that God does as well as to judgment that humans render. It can refer to that final decision making time when all the affairs of the world and those in it are finally recorded by God. It is clear that both the Old and New Testaments understand God to be the only true judge in this final sense. Only God can make an accurate assessment of all affairs. Only God is aware of all the facts and motives behind people's actions. As human beings, we make our judgments based on limited information. 1 Samuel 16:7 reminds us, "For the Lord does not see as mortals see; they look on the outward appearance, but the Lord looks on the heart."

Decision making and discernment stand at the core of the biblical story. From the very beginning, Genesis tells us that God instructs Adam and Eve concerning how to live in the garden, requiring them to discriminate between what they can and cannot do. Our ability to make decisions remains at the very heart of who we are as human beings, created in God's image. Joshua 24 calls Israel to remember again whom they will choose to serve as they are poised to enter the Promised Land. The prophets call Israel to discern and choose as well. Indeed, discernment is a key issue in Jesus' ministry. Those who hear his words and see his signs ask themselves the question "What are we going to do with this man? How do we judge his actions and words?"

"Dokimaso" is the Greek word often used to mean discernment in the New Testament. It occurs (in one form or another) thirty-one times in the New Testament. It can mean "test," "examine," "interpret," or "discern." Its opposite means "reject," such as when Jesus refers to Psalm 118 and the "stone that the builders rejected" becoming the cornerstone in Matthew 21:42 and its parallels. It is sometimes used to indicate a failure to discern (e.g., Rom. 1:28: "did not see fit to acknowledge God"). Often a time of testing is needed for wisdom to appear (e.g., Lk. 14:19: "I have bought five yoke of oxen, and I am going to try them out.").

Paul seems optimistic that discernment (in the sense of "dokimaso") is a gift available to the church and its members. Indeed, some would say that Paul's letters provide something far more valuable than specific answers to particular problems (although he clearly does provide this). Paul is offering the early Christians a way of thinking ethically, a way to make moral decisions. Paul encourages our discernment to be God-centered rather than human-centered. We should not be driven by what the possible human consequences of a decision may be. After all, since the fall, people cannot always know and do what is right (Rom. 1:18; 3:10, 19-20, 23). By nature, people are slaves to sin (Rom. 6:17-20). Rather, we are to live our lives in response to God's gracious mercy toward us and make our decisions as God empowers us (Phil. 2:13: "for it is God who is at work in you, enabling you both to will and to work for his good pleasure"). Discernment then is a matter of faith in God (God will show us the way) and faithfulness to God (that we will follow the way we have been shown). This is a continuing process (Rom. 12:2b: "be transformed by the renewing of your minds, so that you may discern what is the will of God—what is good and acceptable and perfect").

Yet Paul offers more guidelines. The decision making that Paul commends is God-centered and guided by love. Love, for Paul, is the essence of the entire Christian life (cf., 1 Cor. 16:14). Thus love for the neighbor is a way of respecting God's intentions for the world. When issues are not crystal clear, asking the question "What will produce the greatest love?" is one way to follow a God-centered approach. Freedom in Christ for Paul is not license, but liberty to love (Gal. 5:13).

Our discernment must always be embraced with a certain humility, realizing that we are still human and experience God's Spirit in earthen vessels that are fragile and prone to error. Thus we cannot command the same certainty that God does in the discernment process. This is why we discern and God judges in an ultimate sense. But we can acknowledge that God has gifted us as individuals and as a faith community with the capacity for discernment. We can pray for an openness to the Spirit's presence and leading in our lives during times of discernment. We can study God's Word for help on how God has guided the faith community and how it has made decisions in the past. And we can live with a confidence that in the fullness of time, God's will may be made clear for us to follow. Remember Hosea 6:3, "Let us know, let us press on to know the Lord; his appearing is as sure as the dawn; he will come to us like the showers, like the spring rains that water the earth."

When members assemble for a congregational meeting, both a spirit of waiting and receptivity and a willingness to make decisions are needed. Times of silence during debate and decision making can give people perspective. The moderator's role includes attempts at appropriate moments to articulate a sense of the meeting.

Hymns:
> "Come, gracious Spirit" (HWB 303)
> "Gentle Shepherd, come and lead us" (HWB 352)
> "Heart with loving heart united" (HWB 420)
> "Open my eyes, that I may see" (HWB 517)
> "Be thou my vision" (HWB 545)
> "Guide my feet" (HWB 546)
> "Guide me, O thou great Jehovah" (HWB 582)
> "He leadeth me" (HWB 599)

Scripture passages:
> Deuteronomy 30:11-20   Matthew 18:15-20
> Psalm 1   John 16:7-14
> Matthew 16:17-19   John 20:21-23

Visual setting:
> Room arrangement is crucial to the discernment process. People need to see and hear each other. Consider the logistics of breaking into smaller groupings so all may participate.

CONGREGATIONAL MEETING

Opening Prayer

Lord of life,
we thank you that in our worship as well as our
    work
        we can assemble in your presence,
your Son comes among us,
        and your Holy Spirit guides us.

As we meet together in this business session,
come among us, guide us.
        In our uncertainties, give us direction;
        in our differences, give us understanding;
        in our reporting, give us honesty;
        in our planning, give us boldness;
        in our deciding, give us deference.

Never let us forget that we are your servants,
        called to proclaim the reign of God,
        committed to follow Christ in life,
        united as one body in the Spirit.

We are not sufficient of ourselves;
        provide our sufficiency.
We are not wise of ourselves;
        provide our wisdom.
We are not confident of ourselves;
        provide our confidence,
that we may be faithful in your service
        and abound in hope
for the sake of your kingdom. Amen.[91]

BINDING AND LOOSING

It is perhaps the most awesome part of the church's calling to bind and loose, to hold someone responsible for a transgression of commission or omission or to release someone from repented sin (Jn. 20:21-23). Mostly this discipline happens in everyday ways as we make good on our baptismal promise "to give and receive counsel." We all know that self-righteousness is only a hair's breadth away from righteousness and that much anguish has been visited on struggling and sincere people when righteousness became self-righteous. At the same time, there are occasions when people end up in the grip of sin or of guilt. In both cases, the congregation can become the medium of God's grace in binding and loosing.

The following order of service has been adapted from an order for processing an offender's abuse. It will need to be adapted again in various ways to meet the needs of a given pastoral situation. Some acts of reconciliation should be carried out strictly between the penitent and the minister (where the transgression does not involve others or where both victim and offender wish the offender's repentance to be private), others among all those directly involved, and still others with the congregation. In the latter case, a congregational meeting is recommended rather than a public service.

Hymn

Prayer

Lord, our God, great, eternal, wonderful, utterly to be trusted:

> you give life to us all,
>
> you help those who come to you,
>
> you give hope to those who cry to you.

Forgive our sins, secret and open,

> and rid us of every habit of thought that stands against the gospel.

Set our hearts at peace, so that we may live our lives before you confidently and without fear, through Jesus Christ, our Lord. Amen.[92]

L: We have known the mystery of brokenness in our midst.

It recalls to us Paul's confession of his own plight: "I do not understand my own actions.

For I do not do what I want, but I do the very thing I hate.... Wretched man that I am! Who will rescue me from this body of death?" (Rom. 7:15, 24)

We gather here to lament our universal inclination to sin and to lament a specific sin and its consequences.

We gather to uphold the one sinned against.

We gather also to offer forgiveness and reconciliation to the one who has sinned.

Forgiveness has at least two parts, letting go

of anger and not holding the offense
against the offender.

Our capacity to forgive varies greatly and
depends on many factors.

Let all gathered here forgive as they are able
and commit what they cannot yet do to
the Lord.

Because God in Christ forgives, we become able
to forgive. That is the beginning of hope.

"If we confess our sins, the One who is faithful
and just

will forgive us our sins and cleanse us
from all unrighteousness." (1 Jn. 1:9)

Even when we have turned from sin, we
sometimes need to be guided along the
path of repentance,

accepting limits on behavior we cannot
handle.

Where there is a victim, that person needs to
be assured of steadfast love, prayer, and
companionship.

Scripture (Mt. 18:12-22 or others)

*Litany of Lament (appropriate in the case of grievous
offense)*

L: Look, the tears of the oppressed—with no one
to comfort them!

On the side of their oppressors there was
power—with no one to comfort them.

In your mercy, Lord,

P: Hear our prayer.

L: Cry aloud to the Lord! Let tears stream down like a torrent day and night!

Give yourself no rest, your eyes no respite!

Pour out your heart like water before the presence of the Lord!

Lift up your hands to him for the lives of your children. In your mercy, Lord,

P: Hear our prayer.

L: My eyes flow without ceasing, without respite, until the Lord from heaven looks down and sees.

My eyes cause me grief at the fate of all the young women in my city. In your mercy, Lord,

P: Hear our prayer.

L: My soul is bereft of peace. I have forgotten what happiness is. In your mercy, Lord,

P: Hear our prayer.

L: I called on your name, O Lord, from the depths of the pit; you heard my plea,

"Do not close your ear to my cry for help, but give me relief!" In your mercy, Lord,

P: Hear our prayer.

All: Do not forsake me, O Lord; O my God, do not be far from me; make haste to help me, O Lord, my salvation. Amen. (Eccles. 4:1; Lam. 2:18; 3:49-51; 3:17; 3:55-56; Ps. 38:21)

Naming the offense
Words to the offender

Words from the offender
Silence

Pardon

L: Do you turn from your sins and turn to Christ?

Penitent: I do.

L: Do you seek amendment of life and growth in grace?

Penitent: I do.

L: Is it your intention to make good what you have done wrong?

Penitent: It is.

L: The Lord has taken away your sins and will remember them no more.
We will remember them no more. Go in peace and do not sin again.

(Exchange of peace between leader and penitent and with others as appropriate)

Affirmation of the victim (where this is the case, in a simple statement or prayer)

Counsel or discipline (asked of penitent as an expression of his/her intentions)

Litany of hope (the counterpart to the litany of lament)

L: Jesus says, Come to me, all you who are weary and are carrying heavy burdens, and I will give you rest.
Take my yoke upon you, and learn from me; for I am gentle and humble in heart, and

you will find rest for your souls.
For my yoke is easy, and my burden is light.

P: Guide us, gentle Shepherd.

L: My soul is continually bowed down within me. But this I call to mind, and therefore I have hope: the steadfast love of the Lord never ceases, God's mercies never come to an end; they are new every morning; great is your faithfulness.

P: Restore us, loving Parent.

L: By the tender mercy of our God, the dawn from on high will break upon us, to give light to those who sit in darkness and in the shadow of death, to guide our feet into the way of peace.

P: Illuminate us, brilliant Light.

L: What does the Lord require of you but to do justice, and to love kindness, and to walk humbly with your God?

P: Teach us, gracious Wisdom.

L: If we confess our sins, the One who is faithful and just will forgive us our sins and cleanse us from all unrighteousness.

P: Forgive us, merciful Judge.

L: God, who reconciled us to himself through Christ, has given us the ministry of reconciliation; that is, in Christ God was reconciling the world to himself, not counting their trespasses against them, and entrusting the message of reconciliation to us.

P: Reconcile us, compassionate Peacemaker.
L: Love the Lord your God with all your heart,
    and with all your soul, and with all your
    mind....Love your neighbor as yourself.
P: Fill us, great-hearted Lover, with your love.
All:Neither death, nor life, nor angels, nor rulers,
    nor things present, nor things to come, nor
    powers, nor height, nor depth, nor anything
    else in all creation, will be able to separate us
    from the love of God in Christ Jesus our Lord.
    Amen. (Mt. 11:28-30; Lam. 3:20-23; Lk. 1:78-
    79; Mic. 6:8; 1 Jn. 1:9; 2 Cor. 5:18-19; Mt. 22:37-
    39; Rom. 8:38-39)

Blessing
May God bless you and keep you;
May the very face of God shine upon you,
        and be gracious to you.
May God's presence embrace you
        and give you peace. Amen.

(Hymn)[93]

Endnotes

1 All entries that are not otherwise noted were written by John Rempel.

2 Leonard Gross (ed. & tr.), *Prayer Book for Earnest Christians: A Spiritually Rich Anabaptist Resource* (Scottdale: Herald Press, 1996).

3 *Hymnal: A Worship Book* is abbreviated in this Manual as HWB, (Elgin: Brethren Press; Newton: Faith & Life Press; Scottdale: Mennonite Publishing House, 1992).

4 Rueben P. Job and Norman Shawchuck, *A Guide to Prayer for Ministers and Other Servants* (Nashville: Upper Room, 1983).

5 *Prayer Book for Earnest Christians: A Spiritually Rich Anabaptist Resource.*

6 *Daily Prayer: The Worship of God,* (Supplemental Liturgical Resource 5).(Louisville: The Westminster Press, 1987), p. 61. Used by permission of Westminster John Knox Press.

7 Attributed to St. John Chrysostom, HWB, 728.

8 *Wee Worship Book,* (WGRG: The Iona Community (Scotland), 1989), p. 7. Used by permission of G.I.A. Publications, Inc., exclusive agent. All rights reserved. *Please note that this material may not be copied from the Manual without permission from G.I.A. Publications, Inc., phone 708/496-3800.*

9 *Wee Worship Book.* Used by permission of G.I.A. Publications, Inc., exclusive agent. All rights reserved. *Please note that this material may not be copied from the Manual without permission from G.I.A. Publications, Inc., phone 708/496-3800.*

10 *Wee Worship Book.* Used by permission of G.I.A. Publications, Inc., exclusive agent. All rights reserved. *Please note that this material may not be copied from the Manual without permission from G.I.A. Publications, Inc., phone 708/496-3800.*

11 *Wee Worship Book.* Used by permission of G.I.A. Publications, Inc., exclusive agent. All rights reserved. Adapted by John Rempel. *Please note that this material may*

not be copied from the Manual without permission from G.I.A. Publications, Inc., phone 708/496-3800.

12 *Supplemental Liturgical Materials*, (New York: Church Pension Fund, 1994). Used by permission.

13 Translated and altered by John Rempel.

14 Translated by C.J. Dyck in *Spiritual Life in Anabaptism*, (Scottdale: Herald Press, 1996), p. 211. Reprinted by permission of Herald Press. Altered by John Rempel. Hans de Ries (1553-1638) was among the most influential Mennonite leaders in Holland and North Germany in the early post-Anabaptist era. He compiled a book of martyrs, as well as a hymnal, a collection of sermons, prayers, and instructions for the conduct of church ceremonies. He tried to sustain the radicality of the Anabaptist vision while working against the intolerance and factionalism of Mennonites in his day.

15 Translated and altered by John Rempel.

16 *Spiritual Life in Anabaptism*, p. 213. Altered by John Rempel.

17 Arlene M. Mark, *Worship Resources*, Worship Series 12, (Newton: Faith & Life Press, 1981). Material used in this essay was derived from this book.

18 Klaasen and Klaassen, eds., *The Writings of Pilgrim Marpeck*, (Scottdale: Herald Press, 1978) p. 265.

19 *Confession of Faith in a Mennonite Perspective*, (Scottdale: Herald Press, 1995).

20 Ibid., pp. 46-47.

21 John H. Yoder, translated, *The Schleitheim Confession*, (Scottdale: Herald Press, 1977).

22 Helmut Harder, *Guide to Faith*, (Newton: Faith & Life Press, 1979); Bruce A. Yoder, *Choose Life: Becoming Disciples-in-Community*, (Scottdale: Mennonite Publishing House, 1984); Frank R. Keller, *Preparation for Covenant Life*, (Newton: Faith & Life Press, 1979); *Making Disciples: A Guide for Youth Catechism Leaders*, (Newton: Faith & Life Press and Scottdale: Mennonite Publishing House, 1992); Jane Hoober Peifer and John Stahl-Wert, *Welcoming New Christians: A Guide for the Christian Initiation of Adults*, (Newton: Faith & Life Press and Scottdale: Mennonite Publishing House, 1995).

23 *Confession of Faith*, p. 26.

24 Simeon Rues, *Aufrichtige Nachrichten von dem Gegenwartigen Zustande der Mennoniten*, (Jena: Johann Rudolph Kroker, 1743) pp. 132-134. Translated and adapted by John Rempel.

25 *Minister's Manual*, (Newton: Board of Publications, 1950). Adapted by John Rempel.

26 *Patterns and Prayers for Christian Worship*, (Oxford, England: Oxford University Press, 1991), pp. 99-100.

27 Rebecca Slough. Adapted by John Rempel.

28 John E. Skoglund and Nancy E. Hall, *A Manual of Worship, New Edition*, (Valley Forge, Judson Press, 1993) pp. 200-202. Adapted by John Rempel. *A Manual of Worship, New Edition* is available through Judson Press, 1-800-458-3766.

29 Charlotte Holsopple Glick.

30 *Baptism, Eucharist, and Ministry*, Faith and Order #111, (Geneva: World Council of Churches, 1982). The most encompassing process in our time to develop a theology of the Lord's Supper based in the New Testament, guided by tradition, and informed by a wide range of denominational positions is included in this book.

31 John D. Rempel, *The Lord's Supper in Anabaptism: A Study in the Christology of Balthasar Hubmaier, Pilgrim Marpeck and Dirk Philips*, (Scottdale: Herald Press, 1993) p. 62ff; *Mennonite Encyclopedia*, v.5, "Communion," pp. 170-172. This striking turn of phrase comes from Thomas Merton, and expresses in vivid language a reality at the heart of the Anabaptist understanding of the church and communion. For example, in his Programmatic Letters, Conrad Grebel states that in the breaking of bread, the church is one bread and one body; it receives again the oneness which comes from Christ. Communion is the paradigm for the church becoming again what it already is, the body of Christ.

32 This raises the question of the use of eucharistic prayers based on patristic models as they have recently been developed. Many of them have theological and literary depth. We have decided to use them only in highly edited form for two reasons. One of them is that their length and the register in which they are pitched makes

them too lofty for Mennonite use. The other reason is the consistent historical Mennonite pattern of interpreting Jesus' prayers at the Last Supper as separate offerings of thanks before the bread and the cup. When these prayers are combined with a preceding general communion prayer recalling the work of Christ and invoking the Spirit, they give us the fullest combination of Mennonite and ecumenical tradition.

33 It has become commonplace in most forms of Protestantism for churches to welcome all believers who are baptized and live in a relationship to Christ and the church. The believers' churches have found confirmation in churches which baptize infants as a sign of lived faith and obedience. Some people therefore advocate that confirmation be required for participation in the Lord's Supper. Others argue that we must accept communion guests according to the assumptions of their own tradition.

34 John Bell, *Voices United*, (WGRG The Iona Community (Scotland), 1989). Used by permission of G.I.A. Publications, Inc., exclusive agent. All rights reserved. *Please note that this material may not be copied from the Manual without permission from G.I.A. Publications, Inc., phone 708/496-3800.*

35 *Patterns and Prayers for Christian Worship*, p. 76.

36 *Beets Mennonite Prayerbook*, (1802), translated and adapted by John Rempel. See HWB 731-732 for alternative renderings of the Lord's Prayer.

37 Translated and adapted from an old handwritten manuscript copied by J. H. Enns, (early 20th century).

38 Reprinted by permission from *Lutheran Book of Worship*, 1978 (Minneapolis: Augsburg Press), p. 71. See HWB 731-732 for alternative renderings of the Lord's Prayer.

39 H. Wayne Pipkin and J. Howard Yoder, translated, *Balthasar Hubmaier: Theologian of Anabaptism*, (Scottdale: Herald Press, 1989), pp. 403-404. Reprinted by permission of Herald Press. Adapted by John Rempel.

40 Presbyterian Church, Theology & Worship Ministry Unit Staff and Cumberland Presbyterian Church staff, *Book of Common Worship*, (Louisville:

Westminster/John Knox Press, 1993), p. 68. Used by permission of Westminster John Knox Press.

41 Hoyt L. Hickman, Don E. Saliers, Laurence Hull Stookey, James F. White, *Handbook of the Christian Year*, (Nashville: Abingdon Press, 1992), pp. 164f. Used by permission. See HAW 731-732 for alternative renderings of the Lord's Prayer. Adapted by John Rempel.

42 Gail Ramshaw, Eucharistic prayer 5. Adapted by John Rempel.

43 Liturgy of St. James. Adapted by John Rempel.

44 Rebecca Slough. Adapted by John Rempel.

45 Rebecca Slough. Adapted by John Rempel.

46 Keith Watkins, *Celebrate with Thanksgiving*, (St. Louis: Chalice Press, 1991), p. 115. Adapted by John Rempel.

47 Janet Morley, *All Desires Known*, (Harrisburg: Morehouse Publishing, 1988, 1992). Reprinted by permission of Morehouse Publishing.

48 *The Book of Common Prayer*, (New York: Church Pension Fund, 1979), p. 365.

49 *Supplemental Liturgical Materials*.

50 Rebecca Slough. Adapted by John Rempel.

51 *Confession of Faith*, p. 25.

52 Ibid, p. 72.

53 *Book of Alternative Services of the Anglican Church of Canada*, (Toronto: General Synod of the Anglican Church of Canada, 1985). Used by permission. See HWB 731-732 for alternative renderings of the Lord's Prayer.

54 Ibid, includes adapted materials.

55 *Baptism and Belonging*, (North York, ON: The Presbyterian Church in Canada, 1991). All rights reserved. Used by permission.

56 *An Order of Thanksgiving for the Birth or Adoption of a Child*, (Princeton: Consultation on Church Union, 1980).

57 Russell Krabill, *Words for Worship* edited by Arlene M. Mark, selection 276, (Scottdale: Herald Press, 1996). Reprinted by permission of Herald Press.

58 *Supplemental Liturgical Materials*.

59 Excerpts from the English translation of *Ordination of Deacons, Priests, and Bishops*, (Washington: International

Committee on English in the Liturgy, Inc., 1975). All right reserved. Adapted with permission.

60 Elizabeth Stuart, ed., *Daring to Speak Love's Name,* (London: Hamish Hamilton, Penguin Books Ltd, 1992), pp. 120-121.

61 *The Book of Common Prayer,* p. 567.

62 Charlotte Holsopple Glick and Del Glick. Adapted by John Rempel.

63 Rebecca Slough.

64 *Supplemental Liturgical Materials.*

65 Rebecca Slough. Adapted by John Rempel.

66 *A Mennonite Polity for Ministerial Leadership,* (Newton: Faith & Life Press, 1997).

67 Includes material from *Book of Alternative Services of the Anglican Church of Canada.*

68 Excerpts from the English translation of *Ordination of Deacons, Priests, and Bishops.*

69 Adapted from *All Desires Known.*

70 Sources include: *Patterns and Prayers for Christian Worship;* Heinz and Dorthea Janzen, eds, *Minister's Manual* (Newton: Faith & Life Press and Scottdale: Herald Press, 1983).

71 John Rempel, with material from *Minister's Manual,* 1983.

72 Sources include: *Minister's Manual,* 1950 and *Provisional Rite for Consceration of Diaconal Ministers and Deaconesses,* (Chicago, ELCA, 1996)

73 Ibid.

74 *Book of Alternative Services,* p. 563.

75 Ibid, p. 564.

76 Translated and adapted from *Handbuch für Prediger,* (Winnipeg: Conference of Mennonites in Canada, 1965).

77 *Daring to Speak Love's Name.*

78 *Patterns and Prayers for Christian Worship,* p. 147. Adapted by John Rempel.

79 Ibid, p.149.

80 Ibid, p. 159.

81 Ibid.

82 Ibid, pp. 162-163.

83 Ibid, pp. 163-164.

84 Ibid, p. 165.

85 Ibid, p. 157.

86 John Donne

87 *Book of Alternative Services*, p. 554.

88 *The Book of Common Prayer*, p. 456.

89 Sources include: Kenneth A. Gibble, *For All Who Minister*, (Elgin: Brethren Press, 1993), p. 266-267. Reprinted by permission.; Martin Dudley and Geoffrey Rowell, eds., *The Oil of Gladness: Anointing in the Christian Tradition*, (Collegeville: Liturgical Press, 1993), p. 158, 198, 200, 203. Reprinted with permission of the publisher; *Minister's Manual*, 1983.

90 Rebecca Slough. Adapted by John Rempel.

91 Arlene M. Mark. *Words for Worship*, adapted from selection 302. Reprinted by permission of Herald Press.

92 HWB #699, based on a prayer from The Liturgy of St. Basil of Caesarea, 4th century.

93 Melissa Miller. Adapted by John Rempel.

94 From *Confession of Faith in a Mennonite Perspective*, pp. 93-98. Reprinted by permission.

Confession of Faith
Summary Statement

1. We believe that God exists and is pleased with all who draw near by faith. We worship the one holy and loving God who is Father, Son, and Holy Spirit eternally. God has created all things visible and invisible, has brought salvation and new life to humanity through Jesus Christ, and continues to sustain the church and all things until the end of the age.

2. We believe in **Jesus Christ,** the Word of God become flesh. He is the Savior of the world, who has delivered us from the dominion of sin and reconciled us to God by his death on a cross. He was declared to be Son of God by his resurrection from the dead. He is the head of the church, the exalted Lord, the Lamb who was slain, coming again to reign with God in glory.

3. We believe in the **Holy Spirit,** the eternal Spirit of God, who dwelled in Jesus Christ, who empowers the church, who is the source of our life in Christ, and who is poured out on those who believe as the guarantee of redemption.

4. We believe that all **Scripture** is inspired by God through the Holy Spirit for instruction in salvation and training in righteousness. We accept the Scriptures as the Word of God and as the fully reliable and trustworthy standard for Christian faith and life. Led by the Holy Spirit in

the church, we interpret Scripture in harmony with Jesus Christ.

5. We believe that God has **created the heavens and the earth** and all that is in them, and that God preserves and renews what has been made. All creation has its source outside itself and belongs to the Creator. The world has been created good because God is good and provides all that is needed for life.

6. We believe that God has **created human beings** in the divine image. God formed them from the dust of the earth and gave them a special dignity among all the works of creation. Human beings have been made for relationship with God, to live in peace with each other, and to take care of the rest of creation.

7. We confess that, beginning with Adam and Eve, humanity has disobeyed God, given way to the tempter, and chosen to sin. All have fallen short of the Creator's intent, marred the image of God in which they were created, disrupted order in the world, and limited their love for others. Because of sin, humanity has been given over to the enslaving powers of evil and death.

8. We believe that, through Jesus Christ, God **offers salvation** from sin and a new way of life. We receive God's salvation when we repent and accept Jesus Christ as Savior and Lord. In Christ, we are reconciled with God and brought into the reconciling community.

We place our faith in God that, by the same power that raised Christ from the dead, we may be saved from sin to follow Christ and to know the fullness of salvation.

9. We believe that the **church** is the assembly of those who have accepted God's offer of salvation through faith in Jesus Christ. It is the new community of disciples sent into the world to proclaim the reign of God and to provide a foretaste of the church's glorious hope. It is the new society established and sustained by the Holy Spirit.

10. We believe that the **mission** of the church is to proclaim and to be a sign of the kingdom of God. Christ has commissioned the church to make disciples of all nations, baptizing them, and teaching them to observe all things he has commanded.

11. We believe that the **baptism** of believers with water is a sign of their cleansing from sin. Baptism is also a pledge before the church of their covenant with God to walk in the way of Jesus Christ through the power of the Holy Spirit. Believers are baptized into Christ and his body by the Spirit, water, and blood.

12. We believe that the **Lord's Supper** is a sign by which the church thankfully remembers the new covenant which Jesus established by his death. In this communion meal, the church renews its covenant with God and with each

other and participates in the life and death of Jesus Christ, until he comes.

13. We believe that in **washing the feet** of his disciples, Jesus calls us to serve one another in love as he did. Thus we acknowledge our frequent need of cleansing, renew our willingness to let go of pride and worldly power, and offer our lives in humble service and sacrificial love.

14. We practice **discipline** in the church as a sign of God's offer of transforming grace. Discipline is intended to liberate erring brothers and sisters from sin, and to restore them to a right relationship with God and to fellowship in the church. The practice of discipline gives integrity to the church's witness in the world.

15. We believe that **ministry** is a continuation of the work of Christ, who gives gifts through the Holy Spirit to all believers and empowers them for service in the church and in the world. We also believe that God calls particular persons in the church to specific leadership ministries and offices. All who minister are accountable to God and to the community of faith.

16. We believe that the church of Jesus Christ is **one body** with many members, ordered in such a way that, through the one Spirit, believers may be built together spiritually into a dwelling place for God.

17. We believe that Jesus Christ calls us to **discipleship,** to take up our cross and follow

him. Through the gift of God's saving grace, we are empowered to be disciples of Jesus, filled with his Spirit, following his teachings and his path through suffering to new life. As we are faithful to his way, we become conformed to Christ and separated from the evil in the world.

18. We believe that to be a disciple of Jesus is to know **life in the Spirit.** As the life, death, and resurrection of Jesus Christ takes shape in us, we grow in the image of Christ and in our relationship with God. The Holy Spirit is active in individual and in communal worship, leading us deeper into the experience of God.

19. We believe that God intends human life to begin in **families** and to be blessed through families. Even more, God desires all people to become part of the church, God's family. As single and married members of the church family give and receive nurture and healing, families can grow toward the wholeness that God intends. We are called to chastity and to loving faithfulness in marriage.

20. We commit ourselves to tell the **truth,** to give a simple yes or no, and to avoid the swearing of oaths.

21. We believe that everything belongs to God, who calls the church to live in faithful **stewardship** of all that God has entrusted to us, and to participate now in the rest and justice which God has promised.

22. We believe that **peace** is the will of God. God created the world in peace, and God's peace is most fully revealed in Jesus Christ, who is our peace and the peace of the whole world. Led by the Holy Spirit, we follow Christ in the way of peace, doing justice, bringing reconciliation, and practicing nonresistance, even in the face of violence and warfare.

23. We believe that the church is God's holy nation, called to give full allegiance to Christ its head and to witness to every **nation, government, and society** about God's saving love.

24. We place our hope **in the reign of God** and its fulfillment in the day when Christ will come again in glory to judge the living and the dead. He will gather his church, which is already living under the reign of God. We await God's final victory, the end of this present age of struggle, the resurrection of the dead, and a new heaven and a new earth. There the people of God will reign with Christ in justice, righteousness, and peace for ever and ever.[94]

To Will
From KMF

Blessings
CarolSue

Thanks for all your
love, leadership &
friendship.
Aaron, Angela & Maya

Jeanine

Carolyn Ruth

Helen

love, ISAAC

Bruce

Bess

Love + Prayer
Barb

Jenn